D0842516

# Cocktails

Classics and trend-setters with and without alcohol
Delicious recipes for cocktail snacks

Alessandra Redies
Photos by Michael Brauner

BARRON'S

# Contents

## Getting Started .................... 4

Sour, Julep, and Co.—the World of Cocktails .. 4

What's What in the Cocktail Bar: Shaker,
Bar Strainer, and Co. ............................. 6

Drinking with the Eye—a Brief Introduction
to Glasses .......................................... 8

The Strong Stuff: Vodka, Tequila, and Co. ..... 10

Sweets: Liqueurs and Syrups ................... 12

The Other Flavors:
Bitters, Sparkling Wines, and Co................ 14

Tips and Tricks for Shaking and Stirring ...... 16

Hangover Tips for the Morning After ........... 18

## Bartenders' Classics ........... 20

Talking Like a Pro—Bar Speak
from A to Z ....................................... 21

With Bitter Aperitifs............................. 22
With Brandy and Co............................. 24
With Champagne and Sparkling Wine ......... 26
With Gin .......................................... 30
With Rum ......................................... 36
With Tequila...................................... 40
With Whiskey and Rye.......................... 42
With Vodka ....................................... 46

## Bartenders' Favorite Additions ................................. 48

Flavor Kicks: Mint, Lime, and Co. ............. 49

Absinthe .......................................... 50
Cachaça .......................................... 52
Calvados .......................................... 56
Galliano .......................................... 58
Grappa ............................................ 60
Rum ............................................... 62
Tequila ........................................... 64
Vodka ............................................. 68
Shots .............................................. 72

# Low-Alcohol Drinks 74

## Quick to Make and Less Is More 75

With Anisette .................................. 76
With Bitter Aperitifs........................... 78
With Cachaça .................................. 80
With Cognac and Co. .......................... 82
With Ice Cream ............................... 84
With Liqueurs ................................. 86
With Prosecco ................................ 92
With Sherry ................................... 96
With Wine ..................................... 98

# Nonalcoholic Drinks 100

## The Harmony of Juices 101

With Fruit Juices .............................. 102
With Mineral Water .......................... 116
With Tea....................................... 118
With Lemonade................................ 120

# Indexes 124

## 1. Aperitifs

These are generally the drinks that are intended to "open up the stomach" (from the Latin *aperire*, meaning "to open") and accordingly are consumed before eating. They are small in volume, as they mustn't weigh on the stomach. Aperitifs can be short drinks such as an Americano, or even pure spirits such as dry sherry.

## 2. Cocktails

In everyday parlance, cocktails are mixed drinks of all kinds, but for a pro this refers to one of the approximately 30 mixed drinks in a subgroup. A classic cocktail is usually a short drink and thus served in small quantities (2–3 oz. / 6–8 cl). Some cocktails contain only alcohol, and some have a little juice or syrup added.

## 3. Coladas

Classified under Tropical Drinks because of their taste, coladas are mixed with juices and syrups from tropical fruits; for example, the classic Piña Colada with pineapple juice. What really makes a colada a colada, though, is cream of coconut (see p. 49). Another important ingredient of coladas is rum.

## 4. Daiquiris

These belong among the short drinks and are traditionally served in a cocktail glass. One thing is clear—the perfectly classical daiquiri consists of rum, lime juice, and cane syrup, but the proportions in which these ingredients are mixed are subject to great debate. The main thing is to try them and get the recipe for a daiquiri you like.

## 5. After-dinner Drinks

After-dinner drinks are liqueurs that are drunk after a meal in order to stimulate digestion, and thus they are diametrically opposed to aperitifs. Appropriate choices are all cocktails with a sweet base such as the Golden Dream, but even pure schnapps, liqueurs, and bitters are suited to the task.

## 6. Fizzes

Fizzes must be shaken quite forcefully in a shaker to make them fizz. **Collinses** are related to fizzes, but they are stirred in the customer's glass with ice cubes. What these two have in common is that the taste depends on the relationship between lemon and sugar.

## 7. Juleps

These are drinks built around crushed ice, fresh mint, and liquor. Unbeatable as a refreshing summer drink, juleps have one essential thing to watch for in preparation: Use no cheap liquor, and only perfectly fresh mint. Neither dried mint nor peppermint liqueur will do as a substitute!

## 8. Tall Drinks

All mixed drinks made with a greater amount of liquid are referred to as tall drinks. These include such simple mixtures as Gin and Tonic, plus drinks with other liquor / liqueurs that are made with lemonade or fruit juices. The preparation is always the same: Put ice cubes into the glass, then the desired type of alcohol, and pour in the juice or lemonade.

## 9. Sours

These are short drinks (2–3 oz. / 6–8 cl). In addition to lemon juice, to which they owe their name, they generally contain an alcohol base (such as whiskey, gin, tequila, rum, or Aperol) and cane syrup or sugar. Sours are so-called 24-hour drinks; that is, they can be served in-between times or in the early evening.

## 1. Measuring Cup, Shot Glass, or Whiskey Glass

It's easy to prepare a good cocktail; it all depends on the right amounts of the ingredients, so you shouldn't just guess at the measurements and ruin a cocktail by not getting the quantities right. Rather, the most important piece of bar equipment you should get is a metal measuring cup. You can also check the kitchen cupboard to see if you have a whiskey or shot glass that's calibrated in 3/4-oz. and 1.5-oz. (2- and 4-cl) increments. To start off, this is a good and extremely inexpensive substitute.

## 2. Bar Strainer

You don't need to buy a separate bar strainer if you buy a shaker with a built-in sieve (see No. 3), and as long as you shake cocktails that flow easily through the sieve insert into the glass. As soon as you start working with thicker additives, such as fruit puree, the holes of the insert get plugged up and a bar strainer becomes necessary; its slotted, round disk allows thicker liquids to pass through, and the spiral edge keeps the ice cubes in the shaker.

## 3. Shaker

The shaker is the second most important item on the bar accessory hit parade after the measuring cup (No. 1). Even though the pros recommend a Boston shaker (see p. 21), a common shaker with a screw top, available for around $25 in large department stores, will work fine at the start. This has the advantage of saving you from buying a bar strainer, as it has a built-in sieve through which at least the thin cocktails will flow with no problem.

## 4. Ice Crusher

An ice crusher or an ice mill is handy: Put the ice cubes into the top, turn the handle, pull out the drawer, and use the little shovel to remove the crushed ice. Since an ice crusher of decent quality will cost $50 or more, you can also get by with a clean dish towel and a wooden mallet: Pound the ice cubes, and crunch them up in the dish towel.

## 5. Mixing Glass

A mixing glass, or a pitcher or a stirring glass, is needed, as the name suggests, for all cocktails that are not shaken but rather stirred (see p. 16), in order to protect the purity and the strength of the liquor. A good choice is a thick-walled, tall glass with a pouring spout. It's not absolutely necessary to have a glass like this, though; a small bowl, a beer glass, or similar container will work just as well.

## 6. Bar Spoon

On the one hand, a bar spoon with its long, sometimes spiral-shaped handle is useful to stir the cocktail ingredients and ice cubes in the mixing glass (see No. 5). On the other, it can also be used to measure syrups and creams, since these are used in quantities that are difficult to measure with a measuring cup. A bar spoon holds about 3/16 oz. (.5 cl). Good, inexpensive alternatives are a long cooking spoon handle for stirring and a teaspoon for measuring.

## 1. Cocktail Glass

This should hold between 4 and 5 oz. (12 to 15 cl). It can be used for medium and sweet drinks, that is, for medium to very sweet cocktails. These drinks also taste delicious from a classical cocktail goblet, the so-called martini glass. This glass also has a capacity of around 5 oz. (15 cl) and it was designed specially for martinis. It really makes no difference if you use a cocktail glass or a goblet; the main thing is the stem so that you can hold the glass without warming up the cocktail.

## 2. Tall Drink Glass (Highball Glass)

An all-around glass like the tall glass (No. 2) is generally used for serving tall drinks from Gin Fizz to Lemon Vodka and Cuba Libre, but it can also be used for a Caipirinha. One important note: In this book glasses specified for tall drink recipes are meant to be plain, cylindrical glasses with a capacity of about 8 oz. (24 cl).

## 3. Large Cocktail Glass

This is useful when the tall drink glass is too small, for example, for tropical drinks such as a Piña Colada. In this case, use a glass that holds about 10 oz. (30 cl). The shape is a matter of taste and pocketbook. Large cocktail glasses may be simple or more elaborate and expensive as are the "fancy glasses," with rounded, globe-shaped bodies, or stem glasses such as the ones used in many cocktail bars.

## 4. Old-fashioned Glass (Tumbler)

An old-fashioned glass is a glass with a thick base that is available in all different sizes. In this book, a small glass that holds about 5 oz. (15 cl) is appropriate for cocktails. Among the cocktail glasses, this is the universal glass; it can be used very well for a classical Americano or for a trendy Caipirinha. It's even better for drinking straight liquor on the rocks (for example, for whiskey).

## 5. Aperitif Glass

This glass holds 2 to 3 1/3 oz. (6–10 cl) and is best used for classic aperitifs such as the Americano. The classical aperitif glass is most commonly used in Italian cafes, a no-frills, medium-tall glass with a thick base whose diameter increases slightly toward the top. But if you prefer to keep your supply of glasses to a minimum, an old-fashioned glass is a good alternative.

## 6. Champagne Glass

A Champagne class is mandatory for all types of sparkling wine and Champagne cocktails, from the Kir Royale to the Bellini. Even if professional mixers sometimes find it lacking in style to serve Champagne cocktails in sparkling wineglasses, these glasses are fine for use at home. In the appropriate recipes you will find references to the "sparkling wine goblet" or the "sparkling wineglass." These are just suggestions; you can use whatever shape glass you have in the house: glass, goblet, or flute glass. The only essential: The glass should hold 3 1/3 oz. (10 cl).

# The Strong Stuff: Vodka, Tequila, and Co.

## 1. Cachaça

Cachaça is made from sugarcane, as rum is; however, not from processed sugar, but rather from fresh, green sugarcane. Since the production processes are different, there is no comparison in taste between rum and Cachaça. Cocktails such as Caipirinhas prove that sugarcane liquor goes best with lime.

## 2. Calvados

An apple brandy from Normandy, Calvados, like cognac, acquires its character from aging in oak casks for at least two years. It is great not only as an after-dinner drink, but also as a mixer; in cocktails it goes well with liqueurs, juices, syrups, and creams.

## 3. Cognac

Cognac can only be labeled as such if it comes from the Charente region in France. There the wine distillate is processed twice in succession and then aged in oak casks for at least two years. Since good cognac is expensive, brandy can serve as a less expensive substitute.

## 4. Gin

Gin is the basis of famous cocktails such as the Gin Martini and Gin and Tonic. It's among the most popular of liquors. Gin is alcohol that has been distilled several times; in the third distillation, flavorings are added: juniper, coriander, and other plant ingredients.

## 5. Grappa

Grappa is distilled from the residue of the wine *must* or *marc*. Previously considered the "poor people's spirit," grappa has now become a fashionable after-dinner drink and is the basis of several interesting cocktails. The highest-quality grappa usually comes from the Veneto and the Friaul area.

## 6. Rum

Rum is available in a great many varieties. Color and flavor range from light white to heavy brown types. However, rums are all produced in the same way—by fermentation and distillation of the sugarcane juice, molasses, and other materials from sugar production.

10

## 7. Tequila

This is made from the blue agave plants, grown around the small city of Tequila in Mexico. The heart of the agave is used. The fluid is distilled twice in copper boilers. The result is white tequila. If it is stored for several years in oak casks, it turns into brown tequila.

## 8. Bourbon Whiskey

Bourbon owes its characteristic taste—its discreet sweetness and the aroma of vanilla—to aging inside charred oak casks for at least two years. Bourbon consists of at least 51 percent fermented corn, and other grains (for example, rye or wheat), and yeast, which are distilled.

## 9. Vodka

Vodka tastes mild and almost flavorless in comparison to other spirits. That's because nearly all elements that contribute to taste evaporate in multiple distillations. For its production, therefore, the choice of raw ingredients are of minor importance; barley, rye, and potatoes are commonly used.

## 1. Apricot Liqueur

Also known as apricot brandy, apricot liqueur belongs to the large group of fruit liqueurs and to the subgroup of fruited brandies. Fruit liqueurs contain a taste-determining portion of fruit distillate from the fruit that gives the liqueur its name, in this case, from apricots.

## 2. Blue Curaçao

This is one of the orange liqueurs (see No. 6). It is made from bitter orange peels that are steeped in alcohol to release their ethereal oils into it. Clear as water, the liqueur is transformed into Blue Curaçao by blue coloring. It is used in blue and green cocktails.

## 3. Currant Liqueur

This is a classic liqueur that is sold under the label "Crème de cassis." *Cassis* is the French word for black currants, from which the dark red liqueur is made. It is the basis for the legendary Kir Royale. It is used to color and add aroma to many other cocktails.

## 4. Coconut Liqueur

Coconut liqueur can be bought in clear or milky form. In either case it is ideal for mixing; it goes well with almost every other ingredient. It's also tasty straight on ice. It is usually produced from coconut and milk; keep opened bottles refrigerated.

## 5. Liqueur Made from Herbs and Spices

These are embodied for cocktail aficionados mainly by one type: Galliano, an Italian liqueur made from some 70 different herbs and spices. It's the pronounced vanilla aroma of this liqueur that makes cocktails such as the Golden Dream and the Harvey Wallbanger so delicious.

## 6. Orange Liqueur

Orange liqueur owes its aroma to the ethereal oils of bitter orange peels that are released by what's known as the maceration process (steeping in alcohol). After distillation, filtering, and another distillation, water, alcohol, and caramelized sugar are added.

## 7. Curaçao Blue Syrup

Like orange liqueur (see No. 6), this liqueur is produced from bitter orange peels, but is alcohol free. It is used for sweetening and adding aroma. It adds color to many cocktails. It is also used as a basis for alcohol-free mixes.

## 8. Grenadine Syrup

This syrup is made from pomegranate juice, water, and sugar; in cocktails it is essential for a fruity taste and for a gleaming red color. However, be aware that many products that are called grenadine syrup are made from raspberry, strawberry, and cherry juice. When you are shopping, be sure to look at the label!

## 9. Lime Juice

Lime juice is usually also simply mentioned as Rose's, since this typical green bottle is the most familiar lime juice on the market. Produced from concentrated lime juice, water, and sugar, the relatively thin syrup is used not only as a prime ingredient in soft drinks, but also for sweetening and adding aroma to countless cocktails.

13

## 1. Absinthe

Absinthe is a distillate of the wormwood plant. It tastes like anise or licorice. It contains the plant oil thuja, which in excessive doses can lead to opium-like intoxication. While it was prohibited in the past, since 1998 absinthe, with greatly reduced thuja and alcohol content, has again become available. Traditionally, it is used watered down to a 1:5 ratio.

## 2. Anisettes

Anisettes such as Pernod and Ricard were brought on the market after the prohibition of absinthe in 1916. They contain less alcohol (40–45 percent by volume) and no thuja. They have a strong aroma of anise like absinthe. Anisettes are used with water, orange juice, or bitter lemon in a 1:5 ratio. They are also often used in mixes.

## 3. Angostura

For the bar this is an indispensable aromatic bitter. It is made from herbs and spices that include gentian, ginger, and nutmeg. It was invented in 1824 by a German military doctor and intended originally as a medicine. A spirit of angostura spritzer can add flavor to many classic and trendy cocktails.

## 4. Bitter Aperitifs

These contain little alcohol and are great for tall drinks. The leader in this case is Campari, the distinctively red herbal liqueur from Italy. It is closely followed by the reddish orange Aperol made from rhubarb and other ingredients. Quite unpleasant in pure form, in combination with water or juices it makes a pleasantly refreshing drink on hot days.

## 5. Champagne

Champagne is one of the noblest and best-regulated sparkling wines; whatever is designated as Champagne may come only from Champagne, France's smallest wine-growing region to the north and west of Paris. In well-known cocktails, Champagne has been used since the beginning of the twentieth century.

## 6. Port Wine

This comes in white, red, and ruby varieties. They are all the product of different blends, that is, mixes of different grapes from different locations. Whereas white port wine may be sweet or dry, red and ruby ports generally have a sweet, fruity taste.

## 7. Sparkling Wine

Sparkling wine falls into the category of quality wines that sparkle (contain either natural or man-made carbon dioxide gas) and must meet certain criteria. It must have a minimum alcohol content of 10 percent. The basis of a sparkling wine is fresh and slightly sour. It leaves the wine cellar at the peak of its fermentation process, and should not be kept long in storage.

## 8. Sherry

Sherry is a white wine specialty from Andalusia, Spain. There are mainly 10 types of sherry. The most important are Fino (straw yellow, light, and dry), Amontillado (amber colored, soft, somewhat sweet), Oloroso (reddish gold, nutty aroma, semidry to sweet), and Cream (a mixture of Oloroso and sweet wine made from muscatel grapes).

## 9. Vermouth

A wine aperitif, vermouth is, in simple terms, wine mixed with the wormwood herb. There are three taste varieties: rosso, red (brownish red, bittersweet), bianco, white (greenish white, mild, slight vanilla aroma) and dry (fruity).

## 1. Blender

Blenders are especially useful if you want to make drinks for several people. They can help when preparing 10 drinks in a shaker can quickly turn into a stressful situation. If you are not sure whether or not your blender can crush ice cubes, leave the cubes out. Later pour the processed liquid over the ice cubes. The blender also performs well when ingredients such as cream, milk, ice cream, and cream of coconut are added. You can also use it to purée fruit.

## 2. Cane Syrup

Cane syrup gives many mixed drinks a pleasant sweetness. It has an advantage over granulated sugar because it disperses quickly into cold liquids. To make syrup, pour about 2 pounds (1 kg) of granulated sugar into 1 quart (1 L) of boiling water. Stir for a couple of minutes or until the sugar is dissolved and the liquid is clear. Cook the sugar solution a little longer (the longer you cook it, the thicker the syrup becomes), and then let it cool completely. Keep it in a bottle.

## 3. Stirring

This is prescribed for all mixed drinks that are served ice cold and have ingredients that combine easily. It's also appropriate for cocktails that become cloudy after shaking. This happens with many classics such as the Campari cocktail. Also, carbonated ingredients such as tonic water and sparkling wine should not be mixed in a shaker, but rather stirred and added at the end when the drink is put into a glass. If several drinks need to be stirred together in the mixing glass, at first pour a little less into the glasses, and then add the remainder equally.

16

## 4. Garnish

A garnish makes cocktails visually attractive, but shouldn't overload them or interfere with the pleasure of drinking them. So, instead of serving fruit salad and little umbrellas, stick a few tasty, appropriately colorful pieces of fruit on the rim of the glass or on cocktail skewers or spears. Good combinations include pieces of carambola (star fruit) and kiwi fruit or pineapple and banana. Attractive garnishes for tall drinks are lime or orange peels cut into a twist. For those who want something fancier, there are kits including small cocktail umbrellas that are available in liquor stores.

## 5. Ice

Ice contributes a lot to the success of a cocktail. It should be neutral in taste. The ice cubes should not be older than one week; otherwise, they take on the smell of foods stored in the freezer. If you need lots of ice cubes for mixing, buy plastic bags of ice cubes that are available in many supermarkets and liquor stores. And since watered-down drinks aren't very tasty, keep in mind that the colder the ice, the better the drink.

## 6. Shaking

Shaking is the correct procedure for all drinks and cocktails that contain such ingredients as liqueurs, syrups, and egg. All are difficult to mix. To mix you can of course use a blender (see No. 1), but for just one or two drinks, use the shaker. For best results: Shake briefly but energetically for an average of 15 seconds. A cocktail that is cloudy at first should slowly clear up from bottom to top.

## 1. Two Aspirins

Two aspirins the following morning in a glass of water are a trusted way to avoid the effects of a hangover. The tablets will reduce the ache, but will do nothing to eliminate the real causes of the headache (such as dehydration), so also pay attention to all the other tips on this page.

## 2. Exercise

Exercise is the best natural hangover remedy! So after a Friday or Saturday evening that included lots of alcohol, be sure to work out or take a strenuous walk of 45 minutes. Even if it's hard at first to get into the swing of things, afterward, the hangover will be gone!

## 3. Bloody Mary

A so-called "corpse-reviver cocktail," a Bloody Mary works based on the principle that things that have stopped need to be resumed. This is how it's made: In a tall glass (8 oz. / 24 cl) stir over ice 4 oz. (12 cl) of tomato juice, 1.5 oz. (4 cl) of vodka, 1/3 oz. (1 cl) of lemon juice, three dashes of Worcestershire sauce, two dashes of Tabasco, pepper, and celery salt. Serve with a stalk of celery.

## 4. Fruit Sugar

This helps with alcohol reduction and increases the blood sugar level that is responsible for a queasy stomach. The best plan is to start a hangover day with two glasses of orange juice; fresh squeezed would be best. Or you could use powdered fruit sugar to sweeten coffee, tea, or cereal.

## 5. Magnesium

Magnesium is an antistress mineral that fosters alcohol reduction. The first dose should be taken the same evening, the next in the morning, either in the form of flavored tablets or in food. A dose of concentrated magnesium is contained in a breakfast cereal made from oats, nuts, and bananas.

## 6. Milk Products

Milk, cottage cheese, cheese, and yogurt can help prevent hangovers, since they restrict alcohol absorption. So when you plan a party, it's a good idea to eat or drink dairy products and to help yourself to more food, such as blue cheese spread (see recipe, p. 57).

## 7. Mineral Water (or Bottled Water)

This should be drunk in ample quantities during and after every session of alcohol consumption. Alcohol dehydrates the body, which reacts with the notorious shaky feeling. Before you turn in, put a bottle of water next to your bed!

## 8. Prairie Oysters

These are not for everyone, but some people swear by them! For one drink, one would rinse out a cocktail glass (4 oz. / 12 cl) with olive oil. Put in one or two tablespoons of ketchup, and on top of that carefully place a very fresh egg yolk, then flavor with salt, pepper, Tabasco, Worcestershire sauce, and lemon juice and serve with a small spoon. It would be washed down with a glass of ice water.

## 9. Vitamin C

Like fruit sugar (see No. 4), vitamin C is a good accelerator of alcohol reduction that supports the liver as it cleanses the blood. The right choices for the day after are especially citrus fruits, including oranges, and such exotic fruits as kiwi fruits and mangos. They all contain a good amount of vitamin C and fruit sugar.

# Bartenders' Classics

# Talking Like a Pro—Bar Speak from A to Z

*Cocktails have been fashionable for a number of years, although they have existed for around 200 years. Cocktails were invented in the United States, and they spread to England in the middle of the nineteenth century. It's no wonder, then, that many English terms are used, even in foreign languages and countries. Here are some of the useful terms:*

## Boston Shaker
The shaker that the pros prefer, this consists of a glass and a steel part that slips over it and is correspondingly larger. The advantage is that you can see the amounts of liquid through the glass. Note: If you mix the recipes in this book with a Boston shaker, you should increase the quantity of ice by filling the shaker about one-third full of ice.

## Built-in Glass
This means that the drink was prepared in the glass in which it is served. This is the case with tall drinks such as Orange Campari and Gin and Tonic.

## Crushed Ice
Crushed ice is the type of ice that comes from the ice-crushing machine. If you don't have an ice crusher, see page 6 for information on how to get by without it.

## Crusta
The technical term for a rim of sugar around the glass, crusta is the classic garnish for classic cocktails such as a Strawberry Margarita (see p. 41).

## Dash
A dash is the smallest unit of measure used in mixing. One dash is the equivalent of about 1/64 oz. (0.05 cl).

## Jigger
A jigger is a double-ended measure made of steel; one side holds about 1.3 oz. (4 cl) and the other about 2/3 oz. (2 cl). But to start with, you can also use a shot glass with a line measure at the appropriate height for 1.3 and 2/3 oz. (4 and 2 cl) (see also p. 6).

## Ounce
This is the basic unit of measure in mixing drinks. One ounce is the rough equivalent of 3 centiliters.

## Rim of Salt
A rim of salt refers to the salt that garnishes the edge of a glass used for such drinks as a Margarita (see p. 41).

## Stirrer
The long plastic wand that is served along with drinks such as a Gin and Tonic, a stirrer is used to mix alcohol and soft drinks together.

## Strainer
This simply denotes the bar strainer used to hold back the crushed ice or ice cubes when you strain a drink from the shaker or mixing glass into another glass (see p. 6).

### Aperitif **Campari Cocktail**

Ingredients for one drink:
*2 oz. (6 cl) Campari*
*1 1/3 oz. (4 cl) vodka*
*1 dash angostura*
Plus:
*Ice cubes, mixing glass, bar strainer*
*cocktail glass (4 oz. / 12 cl)*

**1** Put the Campari, vodka, and 1 dash angostura into a mixing glass or pitcher with six ice cubes and stir everything thoroughly for six to eight seconds.

**2** Pour the cocktail through the bar strainer and into the glass. Serve immediately.

## *Cocktail Snack*

### *Aromatic Olives*

Serves 6–8
Peel and mince one small onion and one clove of garlic. Simmer four anchovy fillets (from a jar) and one teaspoon of dried oregano in 1/3 cup (100 ml) of hot olive oil. Stir for five minutes. Pour the oil through a fine sieve onto 2 1/2–3 cups (350 g) of pitted black olives. Let cool and serve.

## Aperitif **Americano**

Ingredients for one drink:
*1 oz. (3 cl) Campari*
*1 oz. (3 cl) vermouth rosso*
*1–2 dashes club soda or mineral water*
*1 piece orange peel*
Plus:
*Ice cubes, aperitif glass (3 1/2 oz. / 10 cl)*

**1** Put two to three ice cubes into the aperitif glass. Pour the Campari and vermouth over them. Add the club soda or mineral water.

**2** Squeeze the orange peel over the drink so that the aromatic oils drip into the glass.

### Variation:
If you add 1 oz. (3 cl) of gin you end up with another classic aperitif—a **Negroni**.

## Fruity **Fellini**

Ingredients for one drink:
*1.3 oz. (4 cl) aperol*
*2 2/3 oz. (8 cl) grapefruit juice*
*2 oz. (6 cl) pineapple juice*
*1/3 oz. (1 cl) freshly squeezed lemon juice*
*1/3 oz. (1 cl) almond syrup (orgeat)*
Plus:
*Ice cubes, crushed ice, shaker, bar strainer, tall glass (10 oz. / 30 cl), drinking straw*

**1** Put all ingredients into the shaker along with four ice cubes. Cap the shaker. Shake vigorously for around 15 seconds.

**2** Fill the glass about a third full with crushed ice. Pour the contents of the shaker through the bar strainer and over the ice. Serve the drink with the straw.

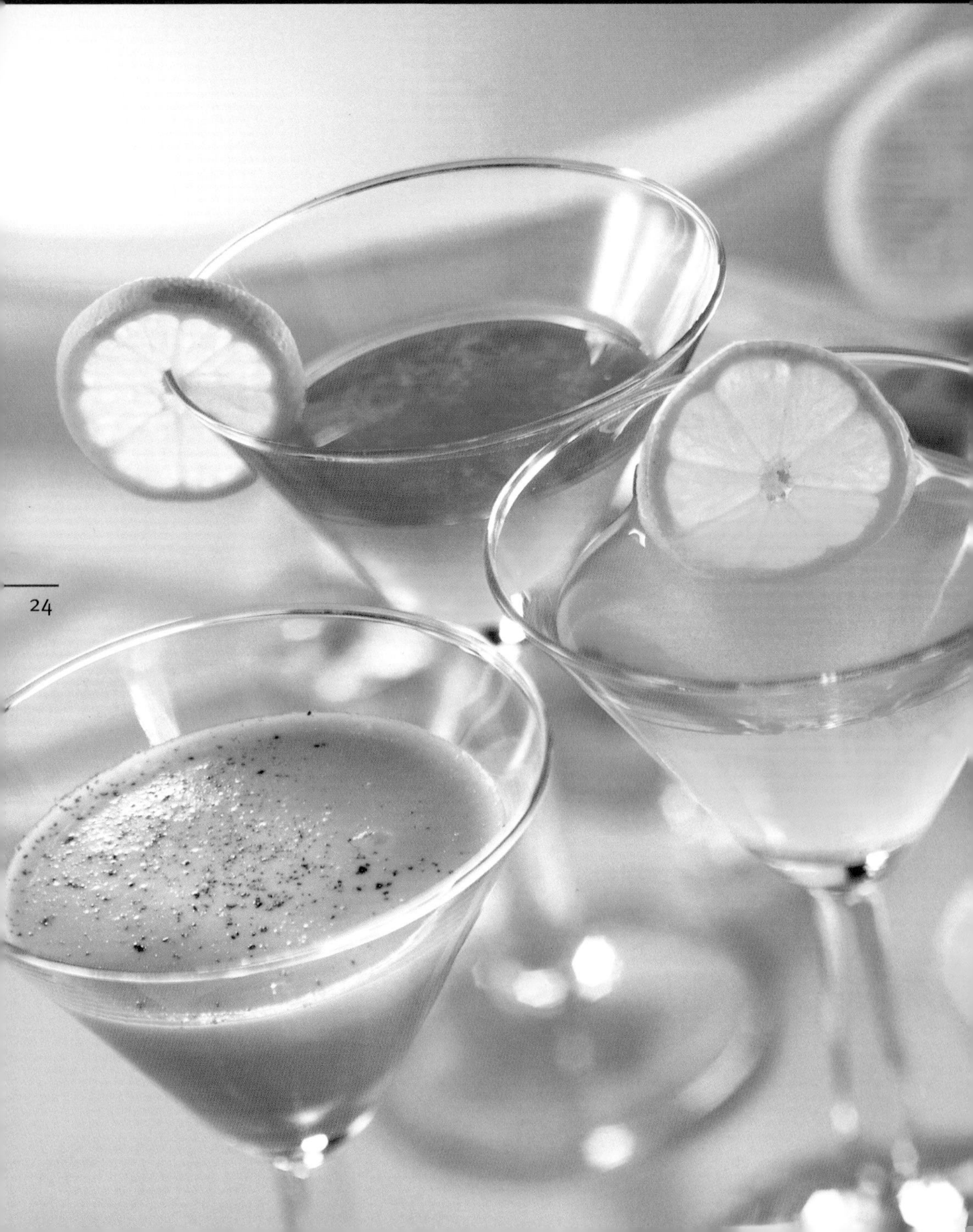

# Creamy **Brandy Alexander**
*(left in photo)*

Ingredients for one drink:
**1.3 oz. (4 cl) brandy**
**1 oz. (3 cl) brown cocoa liqueur**
  **(Crème de Cacao)**
**2 Tbsp. (2 cl) whipped cream or 1 oz (3 cl)**
  **half-and-half**
**Freshly ground nutmeg**
Plus:
**Ice cubes, shaker, bar strainer, cocktail glass**
**(4 oz. / 12 cl)**

**1** Put all ingredients, except for the nutmeg, into the shaker along with four ice cubes. Cap the shaker and shake vigorously for about 15 seconds.

**2** Pour the contents of the shaker through the bar strainer into the glass. Sprinkle a little freshly ground nutmeg over the drink.

## Substitutions:
Not as classic, but still good: Instead of brandy, use **cognac**.

# After-dinner Drink **Sidecar**
*(right in photo)*

Ingredients for one drink:
**1 1/3 oz. (4 cl) cognac**
**2/3 oz. (2 cl) orange liqueur (such as**
  **Cointreau)**
**2/3 oz. (2 cl) freshly squeezed lemon juice**
Plus:
**Ice cubes, shaker, bar strainer, cocktail glass**
**(4 oz. / 12 cl)**

**1** Put all ingredients into the shaker along with four ice cubes. Cap the shaker. Shake vigorously for about 15 seconds.

**2** Pour the contents of the shaker through the bar strainer and into the glass.

# 24-hour Drink **Between the Sheets**
*(center in photo)*

Ingredients for one drink:
**2/3 oz. (2 cl) brandy or cognac**
**2/3 oz. (2 cl) brown rum**
**2/3 oz. (2 cl) orange liqueur (such as**
  **Cointreau)**
**2/3 oz. (2 cl) freshly squeezed lemon juice**
Plus:
**Ice cubes, shaker, bar strainer, cocktail glass**
**(4 oz. / 12 cl)**

**1** Put all ingredients into the shaker along with four ice cubes. Cap the shaker. Shake vigorously for around 15 seconds.

**2** Pour the contents of the shaker through the bar strainer and into the glass.

## Substitutions:
Instead of using brown rum, you can also make this cocktail with **white rum**.

## *Cocktail Snack*

### *Cheese on Skewers*
Makes 20 to 30 pieces
Cut 1 lb. (400 g) Gouda cheese into bite-sized cubes. Wash about 1 cup (150 g) of cherry tomatoes, pat them dry, and cut them in half. Skewer one piece of cheese and one cherry tomato half with a wood or plastic spear.
  **Or** cut up about 1 lb. (400 g) of firm sheep's milk cheese (feta) into bite-sized cubes. Skewer each cube with a pitted black olive on a wood or plastic spear.

**1**

**2**

**3**

## Aperitif **Champagne Cocktail**
*(right in photo)*

Ingredients for one drink:
*1 sugar cube*
*1 dash angostura*
*Ice-cold dry Champagne to fill*
*1 piece lemon peel*
Plus:
*Sparkling wine goblet (3 1/3 oz. / 10 cl)*

**1** Put the cube of sugar into the sparkling wine-glass and drizzle with angostura **(Step 1)**.

**2** Fill the glass with Champagne **(Step 2)**. Squeeze the lemon peel over the glass so that the aromatic oils drip into the glass **(Step 3)**. Add the peel to the glass and serve.

## Aperitif **Kir Royale**
*(center in photo)*

Ingredients for one drink:
*1/3 oz. (1 cl) currant brandy (cassis)*
*Ice-cold dry sparkling wine to top off*
Plus:
*Wineglass (3 oz., 10 cl)*

**1** Pour the currant brandy into the wineglass.

**2** Gently fill up with sparkling wine.

## Substitutions:
You can also use ice-cold dry **white wine** with the currant brandy. This simple variation is no longer called Kir Royale, but simply **Kir**. And if you would like to splurge, use Champagne instead of sparkling wine.

## Summer Drink **Bellini**
*(left in photo)*

Ingredients for one drink:
*1 fresh, ripe peach*
*1 dash grenadine syrup*
*Ice-cold dry sparkling wine to top off*
Plus:
*A blender and a wineglass (3 oz. / 10 cl)*

**1** Wash the peach, pat it dry, peel and slice it. Cut the flesh away from the stone in slices.

**2** In the blender puree the peach along with the grenadine syrup.

**3** Pour the pureed peach into the wineglass and fill the rest with sparkling wine.

## Tropical Drink **Mimosa**
*(not pictured)*

Ingredients for one drink:
*4 oz. (12 cl) chilled Champagne*
*4 oz. (12 cl) orange juice*

**1** Pour orange juice into a collins glass over two ice cubes.

**2** Fill with chilled Champagne, stir very gently, and serve.

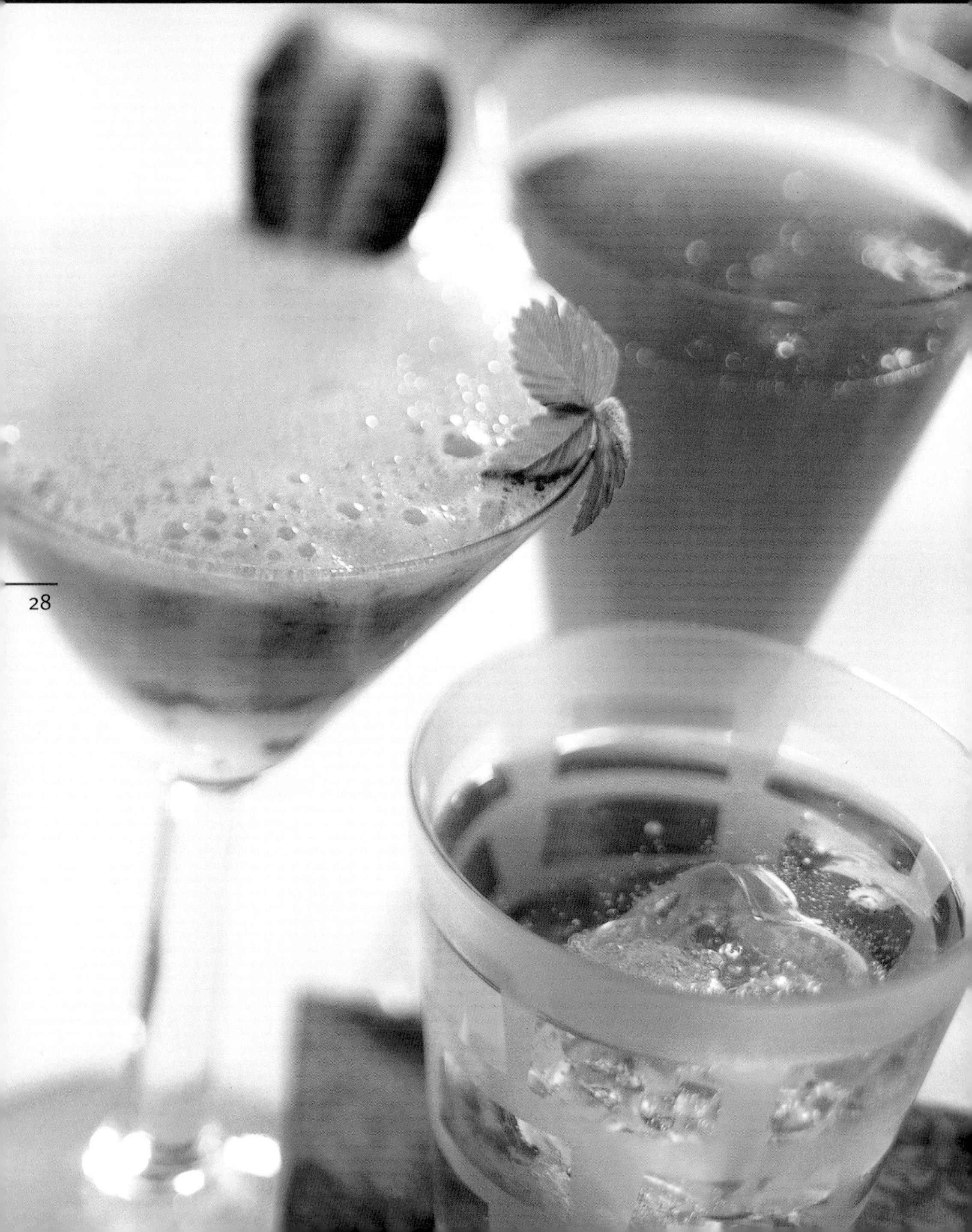

## Aromatic **Prince of Wales**
*(right foreground in photo)*

Ingredients for one drink:
**2/3 oz. (2 cl) cognac**
**1/3 oz. (1 cl) bitter orange liqueur**
   **(Curaçao Triple Sec)**
**1 dash angostura**
**Ice-cold dry Champagne or sparkling wine**
   **to fill**
Garnish:
**2 cocktail cherries, 1 orange slice**
**Cocktail spear**
Plus:
**Ice cubes, tall glass (7 oz., 20 cl)**

**1** Put two or three ice cubes into the glass. Pour the cognac and Curaçao Triple Sec over them.

**2** Add the angostura, and fill with Champagne or sparkling wine. With the cocktail spear, skewer the cocktail cherries and the orange peel. Lay the skewer across the rim of the glass.

## Summer Drink **Portofino**
*(right rear in photo)*

Ingredients for one drink:
**1 1/3 oz. (4 cl) red port wine**
**1 1/3 oz. (4 cl) passion fruit nectar**
**1/3 oz. (1 cl) strawberry syrup**
**Ice-cold dry Champagne to top off**
Plus:
**Ice cubes, shaker, bar strainer, wineglass**
**(5 oz. / 15 cl)**

**1** Put all ingredients except the Champagne into the shaker along with four ice cubes. Cap the shaker and shake vigorously for about 15 seconds.

**2** Pour the contents of the shaker through the bar strainer into the wineglass. Top off with Champagne.

## Summer Drink **Pretty Woman**
*(left in photo)*

Ingredients for one drink:
**4 fresh ripe strawberries**
**1 1/3 oz. (4 cl) pineapple juice**
**1 teaspoon powdered sugar**
**Ice-cold dry sparkling wine to top off**
Plus:
**Blender, cocktail glass (4 oz. / 12 cl)**

**1** Wash the strawberries, remove the stems, and put them into the blender with the powdered sugar and the pineapple juice. Puree for about one minute.

**2** Pour the mixture into the cocktail glass and fill with sparkling wine.

### *Happy Hour*

This wonderful, fruity sparkling wine cocktail is ideal for outdoor summer parties, especially since you can prepare the strawberry puree in advance in any desired quantity. Keep it covered and refrigerated until it's needed. If you have a rendezvous with a Pretty Woman outside of strawberry season, use frozen strawberries instead of fresh ones.

## 24-hour Drink **Silver Bronx**

Ingredients for one drink:
*1 1/3 oz. (4 cl) gin*
*1/3 oz. (1 cl) dry vermouth (white)*
*1/3 oz. (1 cl) vermouth rosso (red)*
*1 1/3 oz. (4 cl) orange juice*
*1 very fresh egg white*
Plus:
*Ice cubes, shaker, bar strainer, cocktail glass (4 oz. / 12 cl)*

**1** Mix all ingredients in the shaker along with four ice cubes. Cap the shaker and shake vigorously for about 15 seconds.

**2** Pour the contents of the shaker through the bar strainer into the glass.

## Substitutions:

You can also use one egg yolk instead of an egg white; in this case, call it a **Golden Bronx**.

## *Cocktail Snack*

### *Cucumber Sandwiches*

Serves 4 to 6
Peel one cucumber and cut it in half lengthwise and then crosswise into thin slices. Add salt and pepper. Take a loaf of presliced white bread. Cut the crust off each of the slices. Spread, over each slice, a mixture of about 4.5 oz. (125 g) of soft butter and minced parsley. Cover half of the bread slices with cucumber. Cover with the remaining buttered bread slices. Cut the sandwiches in half diagonally.

## Semidry Drink **Journalist**

Ingredients for one drink:
*1 oz. (3 cl) gin*
*1/3 oz. (1 cl) vermouth rosso*
*1/3 oz. dry vermouth*
*2 dashes bitter orange liqueur*
    *(Curaçao Triple Sec)*
*2 dashes angostura*
*2 dashes freshly squeezed lemon juice*
Plus:
*Ice cubes, shaker, bar strainer, cocktail glass*
*(4 oz. / 12 cl)*

**1** Put all ingredients and four ice cubes into the shaker. Cap the shaker and shake vigorously for about 15 seconds.

**2** Pour the contents of the shaker through the bar strainer into the glass.

## Refreshing Drink **Gin Fizz**

Ingredients for one drink:
*2 oz. (6 cl) gin*
*1 1/3 oz. (4 cl) freshly squeezed lemon juice*
*2/3 oz. (2 cl) cane syrup / 1 tsp. granulated*
    *sugar*
*1 dash club soda or mineral water*
Plus:
*Ice cubes, shaker, bar strainer, tall glass*
*(8 oz. / 24 cl)*

**1** Put the gin, lemon juice, cane syrup, and sugar into the shaker along with four ice cubes. Cap the shaker and shake vigorously for about 15 seconds.

**2** Pour the contents of the shaker through the bar strainer and into the glass over 6–8 ice cubes. Add a dash of club soda or mineral water.

## Substitutions:
For a Fizz include and mix **white rum**, **whiskey**, and **port wine**.

## Aromatic Drink **White Lady**
*(center in photo)*

Ingredients for one drink:
*1 1/3 oz. (4 cl) gin*
*2/3 oz. (2 cl) orange liqueur (such as
   Cointreau)*
*2/3 oz. (2 cl) freshly squeezed lemon juice*
*1 very fresh egg white*
Plus:
*Ice cubes, shaker, bar strainer, cocktail glass
(4 oz. / 12 cl)*

**1** Put all ingredients into the shaker along with
four ice cubes. Cap the shaker and shake vigorously for about 15 seconds.

**2** Pour the contents of the shaker through the
bar strainer into the glass. Serve immediately.

## Tangy **Paradise**
*(left in photo)*

Ingredients for one drink:
*1 1/3 oz. (4 cl) gin*
*2/3 oz. (2 cl) apricot brandy*
*1 1/3 oz. orange juice*
Plus:
*Ice cubes, shaker, bar strainer, cocktail glass
(4–5 oz. / 12–15 cl)*

**1** Put all the ingredients into the shaker along
with four ice cubes. Cap the shaker. Shake vigorously for about 15 seconds.

**2** Pour the contents of the shaker through the
bar strainer into the glass. Serve immediately.

Garnish:
Hang a curl of **apricot** or **orange peel** on the rim
of the glass.

## Tall Drink **Singapore Sling**
*(right in photo)*

Ingredients for one drink:
*2 oz. (6 cl) gin*
*1 1/3 oz. (4 cl) freshly squeezed lemon juice*
*2/3 oz. (2 cl) cane syrup*
*Club soda or mineral water to top off*
*1/3 to 2/3 oz. (1–2 cl) cherry brandy*
Plus:
*Ice cubes, shaker, bar strainer, tall glass
(8 oz. / 24 cl), two drinking straws*

**1** Pour the gin, lemon juice, and cane syrup into
the shaker along with four ice cubes. Cap the
shaker and shake vigorously for about 15 seconds. Pour the contents of the shaker through
the bar strainer into the glass over two or three
more ice cubes.

**2** Add club soda or mineral water into the
shaker over the leftover ice; swirl the mixture
briefly, and add this to the rest in the glass. Pour
1/3 to 2/3 oz. (1–2 cl) of cherry brandy over this
mixed drink.

## *Cocktail Snack*

### *Chicken Salad*

Serves 4
Skin a roasted chicken (2 1/2 lbs. / 1.2 kg)
from the store. Remove the meat from the
bones, and cut it into bite-sized pieces. Put
the meat into a bowl. In a separate bowl,
make a mayonnaise dressing with 1 1/2 cups
of prepared mayonnaise, 2 tsp. mild curry
powder, 1 tsp. lemon juice, and 2 Tbsp. of
plain yogurt. Mix the mayonnaise dressing
into the chicken cubes. Rinse off a bunch of
fresh tarragon and mix the stemless chopped
leaves into the chicken salad.

The **Martini** (right in photo) is made by combining 2 2/3 oz. (8 cl) gin and 2/3 oz. (2 cl) dry vermouth into a mixing glass with eight to ten ice cubes, shaking the mixture well for about 6 seconds, straining it into a martini glass, and placing an olive in it. In addition to a vodka martini, made with vodka rather than gin, two other popular variations of the martini follow:

# Apple Martini
*(not pictured)*

Ingredients for one drink:
*1 part vodka*
*1 part sour apple liqueur*
*1 part apple juice*
Plus:
*Ice cubes, shaker, bar strainer, martini glass*

**1** Pour all ingredients into a shaker. Shake well and strain into a martini glass.

Garnish:
*If you want to make it look especially attractive, garnish it with a slice of green apple. Enjoy!*

# Dirty Martini
*(not pictured)*

Ingredients for one drink:
*2 oz. (6 cl) gin*
*1 Tbsp. dry vermouth*
*2 Tbsp. olive juice*
*2 olives*

**1** Place an ice cube and a small amount of water in a cocktail glass. Place in freezer for 2–3 minutes.

**2** Fill a mixer with all ingredients including olives. Cover and shake vigorously 3–4 times.

**3** Remove glass from freezer, and empty. Strain contents of the mixer into the glass, include one of the olives, and serve.

## Tangy Drink **Tom Collins**
*(center in photo)*

Ingredients for one drink:
*2 oz. (6 cl) gin*
*1 1/3 oz. (4 cl) freshly squeezed lemon juice*
*2/3 oz. (2 cl) cane syrup*
*Club soda or mineral water to top off*
Garnish:
*1 twist of lemon peel*
*2 cocktail cherries*
Plus:
*Ice cubes, tall glass (8 oz. / 24 cl), drinking straw*

**1** Put all ingredients into the glass, along with three or four ice cubes. Stir vigorously for about 8 seconds.

**2** Pour in club soda or mineral water. Add lemon peel, cocktail cherries, and straw to the drink.

## Substitutions:
Use white rum for a **Pedro Collins**, and brown rum for a **Rum Collins**. Bourbon whiskey promotes Tom into **Colonel Collins**; vodka yields a **Joe Collins**, and tequila a **Ruben Collins**.

## Short Drink **Gimlet**
*(left in photo)*

Ingredients for one drink:
*2 oz. (6 cl) gin*
*1 1/3 oz. (4 cl) Rose's lime juice*
*1 dash club soda or mineral water (to taste)*
Plus:
*Ice cubes, mixing glass or pitcher, bar strainer, cocktail glass (4 oz. / 12 cl)*

**1** Put the gin and the lime juice into the mixing glass along with four ice cubes. Stir vigorously for about 6 seconds. Pour through the bar strainer and into the glass. Add club soda or mineral water to the drink according to taste.

1

2

3

### Fruity Drink **Planter's Punch**
*(right in photo)*

Ingredients for one drink:
*2 oz. (6 cl) brown rum*
*2 2/3 oz. (8 cl) orange or apple juice*
*2/3 oz. (2 cl) freshly squeezed lemon juice*
*1/3 oz. (1 cl) grenadine syrup*
*1 pinch freshly ground nutmeg*
Garnish:
*1 cocktail cherry*
Plus:
*Ice cubes, crushed ice, shaker, bar strainer,*
*large cocktail glass (10 oz. / 30 cl), drinking*
*straw*

**1** Put the rum, the juices, and the grenadine syrup into the shaker with four ice cubes. Cap the shaker and shake vigorously for about 15 seconds.

**2** Fill the glass one-third full with crushed ice. Pour the contents of the shaker through the bar strainer over the crushed ice. Add the cocktail cherry and sprinkle the drink with nutmeg.

## Nonalcoholic variation:
Drivers can enjoy an alcohol-free version of this famous cocktail. For one drink: Put 3 oz. (9 cl) of grapefruit juice, 2 oz. (6 cl) of pineapple juice, 2/3 oz. (2 cl) of freshly squeezed lime juice, 1/3 oz. (1 cl) of cane syrup, and 2/3 oz. (2 cl) of mineral water into a shaker with four ice cubes. Shake vigorously for about 15 seconds. Pour through the bar strainer into a large cocktail glass (10 oz. / 30 cl) over three or four ice cubes.

### Strong Drink **Mai Tai**
*(center in photo)*

Ingredients for one drink:
*1/2 lime*
*1 2/3 oz. (5 cl) brown rum*
*2/3 oz. (2 cl) orange liqueur (Cointreau)*
*1/3 oz. (1 cl) freshly squeezed lime juice*
*1/3 oz. (1 cl) cane syrup*
*1/3 oz. (1 cl) almond syrup (orgeat)*
Garnish:
*2 cocktail cherries, 1 sprig of fresh mint*
Plus:
*Crushed ice, ice cubes, shaker, bar strainer,*
*tall glass (8 oz. / 24 cl), two short*
*drinking straws*

**1** Fill the glass about half-full with crushed ice **(Step 1)**. Quarter the lime and squeeze over the glass **(Step 2)**. Put the piece of lime into the glass.

**2** Put all remaining ingredients into the shaker with four ice cubes. Cap the shaker and shake vigorously for about 15 seconds. Pour the contents of the shaker through the bar strainer into the glass **(Step 3)**. Stir briefly.

**3** Put the straw into the glass and garnish the drink with cocktail cherries and the sprig of mint.

### Creamy Drink **Piña Colada**
*(left in photo)*

Ingredients for one drink:
*2 oz. (6 cl) white rum*
*3 1/3 oz. (10 cl) pineapple juice*
*1 1/3 oz. (4 cl) cream of coconut (canned) or*
*    coconut syrup*
*2/3 oz. (2 cl) cream*
*1 slice of pineapple (fresh or canned)*
Plus:
*Crushed ice, blender, large cocktail glass*
*(10 oz. / 30 cl), two straws*

**1** Fill the cocktail glass about half-full with crushed ice.

**2** Put all ingredients into the blender and mix well. Pour into the glass and stir well. Serve with drinking straws.

38

### Short Drink **Daiquiri**

Ingredients for one drink:
*1 2/3 oz. (5 cl) white rum*
*2/3 oz. (2 cl) fresh squeezed lime juice*
*1/3 oz. (1 cl) cane syrup*
*Lime slice*
Plus:
*Ice cubes, shaker, bar strainer, cocktail glass (4 oz. / 12 cl)*

**1** Put all ingredients into the shaker along with four ice cubes. Cap the shaker and shake vigorously for about 15 seconds.

**2** Pour the contents of the shaker through the bar strainer into the glass. Garnish with lime slice.

### *Happy Hour*

This rum cocktail can also be prepared as a **Frozen Daiquiri**. For six drinks: Put 10 oz. (30 cl) of white rum, 4 oz. (12 cl) of lime juice, and 1/4 cup (2 mL) of powdered sugar into the blender. Fill up with ice, mix thoroughly, and pour into cocktail glasses (4 oz. / 12 cl each).

# El Presidente
*(not pictured)*

Ingredients for one drink:
*1 1/2 oz. (5 cl) light rum*
*1 tsp. grenadine syrup*
*1 tsp. pineapple juice*
*Juice of 1 lime*

**1** Shake all ingredients with ice, strain into a cocktail glass, and serve.

## Party Drink **Cuba Libre**

Ingredients for one drink:
*1/2 lime*
*1 1/3 to 2 oz. (4–6 cl) white rum*
*Ice-cold cola to top off*
Plus:
*Ice cubes, tall glass (8 oz/20 cl)*

**1** Wash off the lime in hot water, pat it dry, cut it in half, and quarter the halves. Put two or three ice cubes into the glass. Pour the rum over them.

**2** Squeeze the lime over the ice cubes and put the pieces of lime into the glass. Top off with cola.

## Summer Drink **Mojito**

Ingredients for one drink:
*1 1/3 oz. (4 cl) of freshly squeezed lime juice*
*6–8 fresh stemless mint leaves*
*2 Tbsp. raw sugar*
*1/3 oz. (1 cl) cane syrup*
*2 oz. (6 cl) white rum*
*1 dash club soda or mineral water*
Plus:
*Crushed ice, pestle, old-fashioned glass*
*(5 oz. / 15 cl), drinking straw*

**1** Put the lime juice, mint, sugar, and cane syrup into the glass. Lightly crush the mint with the pestle. Pour the rum over it and fill the glass with crushed ice.

**2** Sprinkle with club soda or mineral water and stir vigorously from top to bottom. Serve the drink with a straw.

## Short Drink **Margarita**
*(center in photo)*

Ingredients for one drink:
*1 1/3 oz. (4 cl) white tequila*
*2/3 oz. (2 cl) orange liqueur (such as Cointreau)*
*2/3 oz. (2 cl) freshly squeezed lime or lemon juice*
Garnish:
*1/4 lemon, salt (poured into a dish)*
Plus:
*Ice cubes, shaker, bar strainer, cocktail glass (4 oz. / 12 cl)*

**1** Run the lemon section around the rim of the cocktail glass and dip glass into the dish with salt. Remove excess salt by gently tapping the glass.

**2** Put the tequila, orange liqueur, and the lime or lemon juice into the shaker along with four ice cubes. Cap the shaker and shake vigorously for about 15 seconds. Pour the contents of the shaker through the bar strainer into the prepared cocktail glasses.

## Summer Drink **Strawberry Margarita**
*(left in photo)*

Ingredients for one drink:
*1 1/3 oz. (4 cl) white tequila*
*2/3 oz. (2 cl) freshly squeezed lemon juice*
*2/3 oz. (2 cl) strawberry syrup*
*3–5 fresh strawberries (washed and hulled)*
Garnish:
*1/4 lemon, sugar (in a dish)*
Plus:
*Ice cubes, blender, cocktail glass (4 oz. / 12 cl)*

**1** Run the quarter lemon around the rim of the cocktail glass, and dip the glass into the sugar in the dish. Tap the glass gently to remove excess sugar.

**2** Put all ingredients into the blender with four ice cubes and mix thoroughly. Pour into the prepared cocktail glass.

## Party Drink **Tequila Sunrise**
*(right in photo)*

Ingredients for one drink:
*1 1/3 to 2 oz. (4–6 cl) white tequila*
*3 1/3 to 4 oz. (10–12 cl) orange juice*
*1/3 oz. (1 cl) freshly squeezed lemon or lime juice*
*1/3 to 2/3 oz. (1–2 cl) grenadine syrup*
Plus:
*Ice cubes, shaker, bar strainer, large cocktail glass (10 oz. / 30 cl), two drinking straws*

**1** Put all ingredients except the grenadine syrup into the shaker along with four ice cubes. Cap the shaker and shake vigorously for about 15 seconds. Pour through the bar strainer into the cocktail glass over three or four ice cubes.

**2** Pour the grenadine syrup slowly over the mixture. Before drinking, stir the prepared drink in a spiral pattern from bottom to top. Serve with straws.

## Cocktail Snack

### Salsa Mexicana

Serves 4
Wash and halve 3/4 lb. (300 g) ripe stemless beef tomatoes. Cube tomatoes into bite-sized pieces and put them in a bowl. Peel and mince two shallots and add them to the tomatoes. Rinse, trim, and chop two fresh red chili peppers. Add chili peppers to the tomatoes with four Tbsp. of lime juice and stir well. Season with Tabasco, salt, and pepper. Wash half a bundle of coriander. Chop the stemless leaves, and stir them into the sauce. Serve as a dip with taco chips.

## Dry Drink **Manhattan**
*(right in photo)*

Ingredients for one drink:
*2 oz. (6 cl) of Canadian whiskey*
*1 1/3 oz. (4 cl) vermouth rosso (red)*
*1–2 dashes angostura*
Garnish:
*1 cocktail cherry, cocktail spear*
Plus:
*Ice cubes, mixing glass, bar strainer, cocktail glass (4 oz. / 12 cl)*

**1** Combine all ingredients in mixing glass or pitcher along with eight ice cubes. Stir vigorously for about 6 seconds. Pour the mixture through the bar strainer into the glass. Skewer the cocktail cherry with the spear and put into the glass.

## Substitutions:
For a sweeter cocktail replace the whiskey with **Southern Comfort** and the vermouth rosso with dry vermouth to prepare a **Manhattan Comfort**.

## Refreshing Drink **Green Beam**
*(center in photo)*

Ingredients for one drink:
*1 1/3 oz. (4 cl) bourbon whiskey*
*2/3 oz. (2 cl) vermouth bianco (white)*
*1/3 oz. (1 cl) lemon juice*
*1/3 oz. (1 cl) peppermint syrup*
*Ginger ale to top off*
Plus:
*Ice cubes, shaker, bar strainer, tall glass (8 oz. / 24 cl)*

**1** Combine all ingredients except the ginger ale in the shaker along with four ice cubes. Cap the shaker and shake vigorously for about 15 seconds.

**2** Pour the contents of the shaker through the bar strainer into the glass over two or three ice cubes. Top off with ginger ale.

## Aperitif **Old-fashioned**
*(left in photo)*

Ingredients for one drink:
*1 sugar cube*
*1 dash angostura*
*1 slice each of orange and lemon*
*1 2/3 oz. (5 cl) bourbon whiskey*
*Club soda or mineral water to top off (according to taste)*
Garnish:
*1 cocktail cherry*
Plus:
*Ice cubes, old-fashioned glass (5 oz. / 15 cl)*

**1** Put the sugar cube into the glass and drizzle with angostura. Add the slices of orange and lemon to the drink. Press them down with a spoon.

**2** Pour the whiskey over it, fill the glass with two ice cubes, and stir well. Top off with club soda or mineral water to taste, and garnish with the cocktail cherry.

43

## Cocktail Snack

### Bacon Plums

Makes 20 pieces
Halve 10 thin bacon slices (4 oz. / 100 g) lengthwise. Wrap around pitted, dried plums and secure with wooden toothpick. Heat one Tbsp. of oil in a frying pan and fry the bacon plums over medium heat until crispy on all sides. Blot the bacon plums on paper towels and serve.

**Whiskey Sour**

Ingredients for one drink:
*2 oz. (6 cl) bourbon whiskey*
*1 1/3 oz. (4 cl) freshly squeezed lemon juice*
*2/3 oz. (2 cl) cane syrup or 2 tsp. powdered*
*    sugar*
Garnish:
*1 cocktail cherry or lemon slice*
Plus:
*Ice cubes, shaker, bar strainer, old-fashioned*
*glass (5 oz. / 15 cl)*

**1** Put all ingredients into the shaker along with
four ice cubes. Cap the shaker and shake vigorously for about 15 seconds.

**2** Pour the contents of the shaker through the
bar strainer into the glass. Cut the cocktail
cherry, or the lemon slice, in pieces and place
them on the rim of the glass.

## Substitutions:
You can make a Sour with any kind of liquor you
have at home: Besides bourbon whiskey you
can use **Calvados, gin, white** or **brown rum**, and
**tequila**. **Pisco Sour** is also very popular. It is
mixed with pisco, a muscatel grape distillate
from Chile. Another fine variation is the **Aperol
Sour** (see p. 79).

# Rob Roy
*(not pictured)*

Ingredients for one drink:
*1 1/2 oz. (5 cl) Scotch whiskey*
*3/4 oz. (2 1/2 cl) sweet vermouth*

**1** Stir ingredients with ice, strain into a cocktail
glass, and serve.

## Tall Drink **Horse's Neck**

Ingredients for one drink:
**1 twist of lemon peel**
**1 2/3 oz. bourbon whiskey**
**1 dash angostura**
**Ginger ale to top off**
Plus:
**Ice cubes, tall glass (8 oz. / 24 cl),
drinking straw**

**1** Put two or three ice cubes and the lemon twist
into the glass. Add the whiskey and a dash of
angostura.

**2** Top off with ginger ale. Stir the mixture briefly
and serve with the straw.

## Summer Drink **Mint Julep**

Ingredients for one drink:
**Several sprigs of fresh mint (keep one for
   decoration)**
**1 tsp. raw brown sugar**
**2 oz. (6 cl) bourbon whiskey**
**1 dash angostura**
Plus:
**Crushed ice, pestle, large cocktail glass
(8 oz. / 24 cl)**

**1** Rinse the mint in cold water and pat dry.
Remove the stems and put the leaves into the
glass with the sugar and a little water. Gently
crush the mint with the pestle and stir everything together.

**2** Fill the glass half full with crushed ice and stir
until the ice is covered with liquid. Pour the
whiskey and angostura over the ice and stir
briefly. Fill the glass to the rim with crushed ice
and stir vigorously. Put the sprig of mint into
the glass.

45

**1**

**2**

**3**

## After-dinner Drink **White Russian**
*(left in photo)*

Ingredients for one drink:
*1 oz. (3 cl) vodka*
*1–1 1/3 oz. (2–3 cl) coffee liqueur*
*1 tablespoon lightly whipped cream*
Plus:
*Ice cubes, mixing glass or pitcher, bar strainer,
and wineglass (3.3 oz. / 10 cl)*

**1** Put four ice cubes into the mixing glass. Pour the vodka and the coffee liqueur over them and stir well.

**2** Pour the drink through the bar strainer into the wineglass. Top with the whipped cream.

## Variation:

For a **Black Russian**: Stir 1 1/3 oz. (4 cl) of vodka and 2/3 oz. (2 cl) of coffee liqueur with four ice cubes. Pour the mixture through the bar strainer into a wineglass.

## Tall Drink **Harvey Wallbanger**
*(right in photo)*

Ingredients for one drink:
*1 2/3 oz. (5 cl) vodka*
*4 oz. (12 cl) orange juice*
*1/3 oz. (1 cl) Galliano (Italian liquor made with
    herbs and spices)*
Plus:
*Ice cubes, tall glass (8 oz. / 24 cl)*

**1** Put two or three ice cubes into the tall glass and pour the vodka and orange juice over them. Stir well. Add the Galliano and don't stir.

Garnish:
You can garnish this drink with a **slice of orange** or a twist of **orange peel** placed on the edge of the glass.

## Fruity Drink **Los Angeles**
*(center in photo)*

Ingredients for one drink:
*1 2/3 oz. (3 cl) vodka*
*2/3 oz. (2 cl) orange liqueur (such as Grand Marnier)*
*2/3 oz. (2 cl) each of orange juice, grapefruit
    juice, pineapple juice, passion fruit nectar,
    and grenadine syrup*
*1/3 oz. (1 cl) freshly squeezed lemon juice*
Garnish:
*1/4 lemon, sugar (in a dish)*
Plus:
*Ice cubes, shaker, bar strainer, tall glass
(8 oz. / 24 cl), drinking straw*

**1** Draw the piece of lemon around the rim of the glass **(Step 1)** and dip the glass into the plate with the lemon sugar **(Step 2)**. Tap the glass lightly to remove excess sugar **(Step 3)**.

**2** Put the vodka, the orange liqueur, the juices, and the grenadine syrup into the shaker along with four ice cubes. Cap the shaker and shake vigorously for around 15 seconds.

**3** Put two or three ice cubes into the prepared glass. Pour the contents of the shaker through the bar strainer and over the ice. Serve the drink with the straw.

# Cosmopolitan
*(not pictured)*

Ingredients for one drink:
*1 oz. (3 cl) Citron vodka*
*1/2 oz. (1 cl) each of Cointreau or Triple Sec,
    Rose's lime juice, and cranberry juice*
*Lime wedge*
Plus:
*Ice cubes, shaker, bar strainer, martini glass*

**1** Shake ingredients vigorously in a shaker with ice.

**2** Strain into a chilled martini glass. Garnish with a lime wedge on the rim, and serve.

# Bartenders' Favorite Additions

# Flavor Kicks: Mint, Lime, and Co.

*It's the little things that often produce the big results. That's why a martini without a green olive or a Piña Colada without cream of coconut would be only half as good. In the following pages you will find information on these and other flavors.*

## Cream of Coconut

This is usually found in cans in well-stocked supermarkets. The consistency of the sweetened coconut cream varies from thick liquid to creamy firm. It lends to cocktails such as the Piña Colada (p. 39) and the Swimming Pool (p. 68) their exotic touch. If needed, use coconut syrup instead.

## Raw Eggs

In this book raw eggs are used only rarely in mixed drinks. If you use them be careful. They must be absolutely fresh because of the risk of salmonella poisoning! In cocktails such as the Silver Bronx (p. 30), the shaken egg white provides an attractive foam; in the Black Currant Shake (p. 113), the fat in the egg yolk heightens the flavor.

## Lime

Lime is indispensable for gin and tonic and other drinks. It is available in the produce section of all well-stocked supermarkets. Lemons should be used only as a mediocre substitute; limes are far less sour and nearly twice as juicy.

## Mint

Mint owes its fresh aroma to the menthol in the leaves. It is ideal for summer drinks. It releases its cool freshness most effectively in combination with sugar, but that should not lead you to believe that peppermint syrup is an adequate substitute!

## Nutmeg

Nutmeg has a spicy herbal, slightly pungent taste that rounds off cocktails such as Brandy Alexanders (p. 25). An important note: When possible, grate whole nutmegs rather than using ground nutmeg; the former have a more intense flavor than the latter.

## Green Olives

These are standard additions to martinis (p. 35). Their slightly sharp aroma harmonizes best with gin, the basis for this drink. But beware: The best olives are those packed in salt brine, preferably unpitted.

## Cane Sugar

Of a coarse consistency and golden brown color, cane sugar is one important ingredient of Caipirinhas, Mojitos, or similar drinks. Replace this with white refined sugar or cane syrup only in emergency cases as the taste is completely different!

## Cream

Cream gives after-dinner drinks such as the Golden Dream (p. 59) their typically creamy consistency. It also softens the sharp taste of strong spirits. Drink cream cocktails with care as their sweetened taste makes them seem to contain less alcohol than they actually do.

## Lemon Juice

Lemon juice should be freshly squeezed rather than from the bottle. An important detail: Squeeze the lemon right before mixing the drink.

## Tall Drink **Absinthe Sunset**
*(right in photo)*

Ingredients for one drink:
*1 oz. (3 cl) absinthe (55 percent vol.)*
*2/3 oz. black currant liqueur (cassis)*
*1 dash Rose's lime juice*
*Clear lemon-flavored soft drink to top off*
Plus:
*Crushed ice, tall glass (8 oz. / 24 cl),*
*drinking straw*

1 Fill the glass about halfway with crushed ice. Pour first the absinthe and then the black currant liqueur over it. Add the lime juice.

2 Top off with lemon-flavored soft drink. Serve the drink with a straw.

## Refreshing **Green Ice Fairy**
*(middle in photo)*

Ingredients for one drink:
*1 oz. (3 cl) absinthe (55 percent vol.)*
*2/3 oz. (2 cl) freshly squeezed lemon juice*
*1/2 oz. (1.5 cl) Rose's lime juice*
*1 teaspoon granulated sugar*
Plus:
*Crushed ice, old-fashioned glass (5 oz. /*
*15 cl), drinking straw*

1 Fill the glass about three-quarters full with crushed ice. Add first the lemon juice, then the lime juice, and finally the absinthe.

2 Sprinkle with the sugar and stir well. Serve the drink with the straw.

## Substitutions:
If you don't like the high alcohol content of the absinthe, you can mix the Green Ice Fairy with **Anisette** (for example, Pernod or Ricard).

## Strong Drink **Sazerac**
*(left in photo)*

Ingredients for one drink:
*2/3 oz. (2 cl) absinthe (55 percent vol.)*
*2 oz. (6 cl) bourbon whiskey*
*1–2 teaspoons refined sugar*
*3 drops angostura*
Garnish:
*1 twist of lemon peel*
Plus:
*Ice cubes, shaker, bar strainer, cocktail glass*
*(4 oz. / 12 cl)*

1 Pour the absinthe into the cocktail glass and swirl the glass to allow the absinthe to coat the whole inside of the glass.

2 Put the whiskey, sugar, and angostura into the shaker along with four ice cubes. Cap the shaker and shake vigorously for about 15 seconds. Pour through the bar strainer into the prepared glass.

51

3 Add the lemon peel and serve the drink at once.

## *Cocktail Snack*

### *Meatballs*

Serves 4–6
Peel and chop one onion. Mix the chopped onion with approximately 1 lb. (500 g) of mixed ground meat, 1/2 cup (50 g) of bread crumbs, 1/3 cup (1 cl) half-and-half, one egg, and the grated peel of half a lemon. Add salt and pepper, and mix thoroughly. Shape 18 balls by hand. Over medium heat, in 2 Tbsp. of oil, fry them golden-brown on both sides. Drain.

## Fruity Drink **Latin Lover**

*(center in photo)*

Ingredients for one drink:
*2/3 oz. (2 cl) each Cachaça and white tequila*
*1 2/3 oz. (5 cl) pineapple juice*
*1/3 oz. (1 cl) freshly squeezed lemon juice*
*2/3 oz. (2 cl) Rose's lime juice*
Plus:
*Ice cubes, crushed ice, shaker, bar strainer,*
*tall glass (8 oz. / 24 cl)*

**1** Combine all ingredients in the shaker along with four ice cubes. Cap the shaker and shake vigorously for about 15 seconds.

**2** Fill the glass about a third full with crushed ice. Pour the contents of the shaker through the strainer and over the ice.

## Sweet Drink **Peppermint Patty**

*(right in photo)*

Ingredients for one drink:
*1 oz. (3 cl) Cachaça*
*1 1/3 oz. (4 cl) pineapple juice*
*1 oz. (3 cl) coconut syrup*
*1/3 oz. (1 cl) peppermint syrup*
Plus:
*Ice cubes, crushed ice, shaker, bar strainer,*
*tall glass (7 oz. / 20 cl)*

**1** Put all ingredients into the shaker with four ice cubes. Cap the shaker and shake vigorously for about 15 seconds.

**2** Fill the glass about one-third full with crushed ice and pour the contents of the shaker through the strainer over the ice.

## Summer Drink **Caipirinha**

*(left in photo)*

Ingredients for one drink:
*1 lime*
*2 oz. (6 cl) Cachaça*
*2–3 tsp. brown cane sugar*
Plus:
*Crushed ice, pestle, old-fashioned glass*
*(5 oz. / 15 cl), two short drinking straws*

**1** Wash the lime in hot water, pat it dry, quarter it, and put it into the glass. Add the cane sugar. Squeeze out the lime juice with the pestle **(Step 1)**.

**2** Fill the glass with crushed ice **(Step 2)** and pour the Cachaça over it **(Step 3)**. Stir thoroughly and serve with the drinking straws.

## Substitutions:

If you don't have any Cachaça available but have a sudden urge for a Caipirinha, you can prepare this cocktail with **vodka** making a **Caipirovka** (see p. 71), or with **white rum**. Otherwise, pour **apple corn schnapps** over the lime. Camparinha, which is made with **campari**, the Italian herb liqueur, is very trendy right now. For an **Asiatic version** of this drink: Use two or three stalks of lemon grass instead of the lime. Wash the lemon grass stalks, and cut the white lower parts into pieces one inch (2.5 cm) long. Add them to the mixture in the glass and sprinkle with cane sugar as described above.

### Fruity Drink **Cherry Lips**

Ingredients for one drink:
*1 oz. (3 cl) Cachaça*
*1 oz. (3 cl) vodka*
*2 2/3 oz. (8 cl) cherry nectar*
*1/3 oz. (1 cl) freshly squeezed lemon juice*
*1/3 oz. (1 cl) cane syrup*
Plus:
*Ice cubes, blender, bar strainer, large cocktail glass (10 oz. / 30 cl)*

**1** Put all ingredients along with the cocktail cherries and three ice cubes into the blender. Mix thoroughly until the ice cubes are crushed.

**2** Pour the contents of the blender through the bar strainer over two or three ice cubes in the glass.

### Tart Drink **Frogman**

Ingredients for one drink:
*1 oz. (3 cl) Cachaça*
*2/3 oz. (2 cl) freshly squeezed lime juice*
*2/3 oz. (2 cl) Rose's lime juice*
*2/3 oz. (2/3 cl) green peppermint syrup*
Plus:
*Ice cubes, shaker, bar strainer, cocktail glass (4 oz. / 12 cl)*

**1** Put all ingredients and four ice cubes into the shaker. Cap the shaker and shake vigorously for about 15 seconds.

**2** Pour the contents of the shaker through the bar strainer into the glass.

Strong Drink **Wild Thing**

Ingredients for one drink:
*2/3 oz. (2 cl) Cachaça*
*2/3 oz. (2 cl) white tequila*
*2/3 oz. (2 cl) white rum*
*1 1/3 oz. (4 cl) pineapple juice*
*1 1/3 oz. (4 cl) orange juice*
*2/3 oz. (2 cl) Rose's lime juice*
*1/3 oz. (1 cl) cane syrup*
Garnish:
*1 slice orange*
Plus:
*Ice cubes, shaker, bar strainer, tall glass*
*(8 oz. / 24 cl), two drinking straws*

**1** Put all ingredients into the shaker with four ice cubes. Cap the shaker and shake vigorously for about 15 seconds.

**2** Pour the contents of the shaker through the strainer into the tall glass. Cut the orange slice partially in half and stick it onto the rim of the glass. Serve the drink with the straws.

## Substitutions:

For a tangier flavor substitute 2 2/3 oz. (8 cl) of **grapefruit juice** for the orange and pineapple juice. Garnish with a twist of grapefruit peel, making the twist with a peeler, and stick it onto the rim of the glass.

## Garnish:

For a fancier garnish: Cut the **orange slice** partially in half in the center, twist the ends, and stick a cocktail spear through them. Add one cocktail cherry on each side and lay the spear on the rim of the glass.

## Aperitif **Double Apple**

*(center in photo)*

Ingredients for one drink:
*1 oz. (3 cl) Calvados*
*2/3 oz. (2 cl) apple juice*
*1/3 oz. (1 cl) freshly squeezed lime juice*
*1/3 oz. (1 cl) maple syrup*
Plus:
*Ice cubes, shaker, bar strainer, cocktail glass*
*(4 oz. / 12 cl)*

**1** Put all ingredients into the shaker with four ice cubes. Cap the shaker and shake vigorously for about 15 seconds.

**2** Pour the contents of the shaker through the bar strainer into the glass.

## Refreshing **Tropical Apple**

*(left in photo)*

Ingredients for one drink:
*1 1/3 oz. (4 cl) Calvados*
*2/3 oz. (2 cl) white rum*
*2/3 oz. (2 cl) freshly squeezed lime juice*
*1/3 oz. (1 cl) almond syrup (orgeat)*
*1/3 oz. (1 cl) cane syrup*
*1/2 lime*
Plus:
*Crushed ice, shaker, bar strainer, tall glass*
*(8 oz / 24 cl), drinking straw*

**1** Put the Calvados, rum, lime juice, and syrups into the shaker with four ice cubes. Cap the shaker and shake vigorously for about 15 seconds.

**2** Fill a tall glass about half full with crushed ice. Quarter the lime and squeeze the pieces over the ice. Put the lime pieces into the glass. Pour the contents of the shaker through the bar strainer over the ice. Serve with the drinking straw.

## Party Drink **Red Pleasure**

*(right in photo)*

Ingredients for one drink:
*2/3 oz. (2 cl) Calvados*
*2/3 oz. (2 cl) vodka*
*2/3 oz. (2 cl) gin*
*1 1/3 oz. (4 cl) orange juice*
*1 dash freshly squeezed lemon juice*
*2/3 oz. (2 cl) grenadine syrup*
Plus:
*Crushed ice, tall glass (8 oz / 24 cl),*
*drinking straw*

**1** Fill the tall glass about half full with crushed ice. Pour the Calvados, vodka, gin, orange juice, and lemon juice over the ice. Stir well.

**2** Add the grenadine syrup. Fill the glass nearly to the rim with crushed ice and stir thoroughly. Serve the drink with the straw.

57

## *Cocktail Snack*

### *Ranch House Pecans*

Serves 4–6
Preheat oven to 300°F (150°C). Pour 2 Tbsp. melted butter into an ovenproof dish. Add 2 Tbsp. Worcestershire sauce, a few drops of Tabasco, 1 tsp. chili pepper, 1/2 tsp. curry powder, and salt. Mix well. Add 1 1/2 cup (200 g) of shelled pecans and stir well. Bake in the oven (middle rack) at 285°F (140°C in a convection oven) for about 30 minutes and stir occasionally. Let cool and serve.

58

### Strong Drink **Yellow Chief**

Ingredients for one drink:
*1 oz. (3 cl) Galliano (Italian herb and spice liqueur)*
*1 oz. (3 cl) white rum*
*1/3 oz. (1 cl) apricot brandy (apricot-flavored liqueur)*
*2 2/3 oz. (8 cl) pineapple juice*
*1/3 oz. (1 cl) freshly squeezed lime juice*
*1/3 oz. (1 cl) cane syrup*
Plus:
*Ice cubes, shaker, bar strainer, tall glass (8 oz. / 24 cl)*

**1** Put all ingredients into the shaker along with four ice cubes. Cap the shaker and shake vigorously for about 15 seconds.

**2** Pour the contents of the shaker through the bar strainer over two or three ice cubes in the glass.

## *Cocktail Snack*

### *Papaya Morsels*

Serves 4
Quarter one ripe papaya. Remove the pit with a spoon. Peel the papaya quarters with a knife. Cube the flesh of the fruit, and drizzle with 2 Tbsp. of lemon juice. Cut 4 very thin slices of prosciutto lengthwise into fairly long strips about 1 inch (3 cm) long. Wrap the papaya pieces in the prosciutto and season with a little black pepper. Skewer the morsels with a wooden spear.

## Tropical Drink **Yellow Bird**

Ingredients for one drink:
*1 oz. (3 cl) brown rum*
*1 oz. (3 cl) banana liqueur (Crème de Bananes)*
*2/3 oz. (2 cl) Galliano*
*1 1/3 oz. (4 cl) orange juice*
*1 1/3 oz. (4 cl) pineapple juice*
Plus:
*Ice cubes, shaker, bar strainer, tall glass*
*(8 oz. / 24 cl), two drinking straws*

**1** Put all ingredients into the shaker with four ice cubes. Cap the shaker and shake vigorously for about 15 seconds.

**2** Pour the contents of the shaker through the bar strainer into the glass over two or three ice cubes. Serve with the drinking straws.

## After-dinner Drink **Golden Dream**

Ingredients for one drink:
*1 oz. (3 cl) orange liqueur*
*1/3 oz. (1 cl) Galliano*
*1 1/3 oz. (4 cl) orange juice*
*1 oz. (3 cl) light cream*
Plus:
*Ice cubes, shaker, bar strainer, cocktail glass*
*(4 oz. / 12 cl)*

**1** Put all the ingredients into the shaker with four ice cubes. Cap the shaker and shake vigorously for about 15 seconds.

**2** Pour the contents of the shaker through the bar strainer into the glass.

## Aperitif **Green Moon**

*(front in photo)*

Ingredients for one drink:
*1 oz. (3 cl) grappa (Italian clear distillate)*
*2/3 oz. (2 cl) orange liqueur (such as Cointreau)*
*2/3 oz. (2 cl) Rose's lime juice*
*1 dash peppermint syrup*
Garnish:
*A few fresh mint leaves*
Plus:
*Ice cubes, shaker, bar strainer, cocktail glass (4 oz. / 12 cl)*

**1** Put all the ingredients into the shaker with four ice cubes. Cap the shaker and shake vigorously for about 15 seconds.

**2** Pour the contents of the shaker through the bar strainer into the glass. Add a few mint leaves to the drink and serve at once.

## Party Drink **Sandy's Sofa Surfer**

*(center in photo)*

Ingredients for one drink:
*1 1/3 oz. (4 cl) dry white wine*
*2/3 oz. (2 cl) grappa*
*1/3 ounce (1 cl) black currant liqueur (cassis)*
*2/3 oz. (2 cl) Rose's lime juice*
Plus:
*Ice cubes, shaker, bar strainer, cocktail glass (4 oz. / 12 cl)*

**1** Put all ingredients into the shaker with four ice cubes. Cap the shaker and shake vigorously for about 15 seconds.

**2** Pour the contents of the shaker through the bar strainer into the glass.

## Garnish:

Hang a cluster of fresh black currants on the edge of the glass, or stick a grape that's been cut into a partial half onto the rim of the glass.

## Strong **Old Gondolier**

*(rear in photo)*

Ingredients for one drink:
*1 1/2 oz. (4.5 cl) grappa*
*1/2 oz. (1.4 cl) peppermint liqueur (Crème de Menthe)*
*1 dash Blue Curaçao*
Plus:
*Ice cubes, shaker, bar strainer, cocktail glass (4 oz. / 12 cl)*

**1** Put all ingredients into the shaker with four ice cubes. Cap the shaker and shake vigorously for about 15 seconds.

**2** Pour the contents of the shaker through the bar strainer into the glass.

## *Cocktail Snack*

### *Tuna Crostini*

Serves 4
Wash half a bunch of parsley and pat dry. Peel two cloves of garlic and mince with the stemless parsley. Drain 6-oz. (175-g) can of tuna in oil and puree with 1/3 cup (50 g) Ricotta cheese. Stir in the parsley-garlic mixture. Flavor with 2 tsp. of lemon juice, salt, and pepper. Toast four slices of white bread. Spread the slices with the tuna and flavor to taste with sliced olives.

Fruity Drink **Tame Zombie**

Ingredients for one drink:
*2/3 oz. (2 cl) each brown and white rum*
*2/3 oz. (2 cl) orange liqueur (such as Cointreau)*
*1 1/3 oz. (4 cl) each orange juice and pineapple juice*
*1/3–2/3 oz. (1–2 cl) freshly squeezed lemon juice*
*2/3 oz. (2 cl) grenadine syrup*
Plus:
*Crushed ice, ice cubes, shaker, bar strainer, large cocktail glass (10 oz. / 30 cl), two drinking straws*

**1** Fill the glass about one-third full with crushed ice. Put all ingredients into the shaker with four ice cubes. Cap the shaker and shake vigorously for about 15 seconds.

**2** Pour the contents of the shaker through the strainer into the glass and stir. Serve with the straw.

## Variation:

If you want a classic—that is, a **strong Zombie**—use: 2 oz. (6 cl) brown rum, 2/3 oz. (2 cl) high-proof (73 percent vol.) brown rum, 2/3 oz. (2 cl) white rum, 2/3 oz. (2 cl) orange liqueur, 1 1/3 oz. (4 cl) freshly squeezed lemon juice, 2/3 oz. (2 cl) orange juice, and two or three dashes of grenadine syrup. Shake all the ingredients in the shaker and pour over crushed ice.

## *Cocktail Snack*

### *Blue Cheese Spread*

Serves 4–6
With a fork mix together 3 1/2 oz. (100 g) of Roquefort or Gorgonzola cheese with about 3 Tbsp. fresh cream cheese and 1/3 cup (a small block) of soft butter. Flavor with a few drops of Worcestershire sauce and salt and pepper. Serve with crackers.

## Strong Drink **Long Island Iced Tea**

Ingredients for one drink:
*1/3 oz. (1 cl) tequila*
*1/3 oz. (1 cl) brown rum*
*1/3 oz. (1 cl) vodka*
*1/3 oz. (1 cl) gin*
*1/3 oz. (1 cl) orange liqueur (such as Cointreau)*
*1/3 oz. (1 cl) freshly squeezed lime juice*
*2/3 oz. (2 cl) orange juice*
*Ice-cold cola to top off*
Plus:
*Ice cubes, shaker, bar strainer, tall glass*
*(8 oz. / 24 cl), two drinking straws*

**1** Put all ingredients except the cola into the shaker with four ice cubes. Cap the shaker and shake vigorously for about 15 seconds.

**2** Put two or three ice cubes into the glass. Pour the contents of the shaker through the bar strainer and over the ice. Top off with cola. Serve with drinking straws.

63

## Substitutions:

If your home bar is not quite as well stocked, mix the Long Island Iced Tea this way: Combine 2/3 oz. (2 cl) each vodka, gin, white rum, and orange liqueur with lemon and orange juices in the shaker. Shake with four ice cubes. Pour through the bar strainer into a glass, and top off with ice-cold cola.

## Garnish:

Wash one **carambola** (star fruit). Pat it dry, and slice it horizontally through the middle. Decorate the cocktail by hanging one slice on the rim of the glass. Grass-green drinking straws can make a good addition (see photo).

64

**1**

**2**

**3**

## Aromatic Drink **Kahlúa Tropical**
*(left in photo)*

Ingredients for one drink:
*2/3 oz. (2 cl) tequila*
*2/3 oz. (2 cl) coffee liqueur (such as Kahlúa)*
*2 oz. (6 cl) orange juice*
*2 oz. (6 cl) passion fruit nectar*
*1/3 oz. (1 cl) freshly squeezed lemon juice*
*2/3 oz. (2 cl) grenadine syrup*
Plus:
*Ice cubes, shaker, bar strainer, large cocktail glass (10 oz. / 30 cl), two drinking straws*

**1** Put all ingredients into the shaker with four ice cubes. Cap the shaker and shake vigorously for about 15 seconds.

**2** Pour the contents of the shaker into the glass over two or three ice cubes. Serve with the straws.

## Tall Drink **Tequassis**
*(center in photo)*

Ingredients for one drink:
*1 lime*
*1 2/3 oz. (5 cl) tequila*
*2/3 oz. (2 cl) black currant liqueur (cassis)*
*Ice-cold ginger ale to top off*
Plus:
*Crushed ice, old-fashioned glass (5 oz. / 15 cl), two short drinking straws*

**1** Fill the glass about half-full with crushed ice. Wash the lime, pat it dry, cut it into eighths, and squeeze it over the ice. Put the pieces of lime into the glass.

**2** Pour the tequila and the black currant liqueur into the glass. Top off with ginger ale. Stir briefly and serve with the straws.

## Summer Drink **Blue Ocean**
*(right in photo)*

Ingredients for one drink:
*1 oz. (3 cl) white tequila*
*1 oz. (3 cl) Blue Curaçao*
*2 oz. (6 cl) grapefruit juice*
*1/3 ounce (1 cl) passion fruit syrup*
*3 thin slices of fresh lemon*
*3 cocktail cherries*
*1 1/3 oz. (4 cl) clear lemonade*
Plus:
*Ice cubes, shaker, bar strainer, large cocktail glass (10 oz. / 30 cl), two drinking straws*

**1** Combine the tequila, Blue Curaçao, grapefruit juice, and passion fruit syrup into the shaker with four ice cubes. Cap the shaker and shake vigorously for about 15 seconds.

**2** Add two or three ice cubes, three thin lemon slices, and three cocktail cherries to the glass **(Step 1)**. Pour the contents of the shaker through the bar strainer and over them.

**3** Pour the lemonade over the ice remaining in the shaker **(Step 2)**. Swirl the cocktail around, and pour it through the bar strainer into the glass. Put the two drinking straws into the glass and gently stir the drink **(Step 3)**.

## Substitutions:
Instead of using passion fruit syrup, try mixing this delicious drink with **grenadine syrup**. Serve it as a **Red Ocean**.

## Fruity Drink **King Midas**
*(left in photo)*

Ingredients for one drink:
*1 1/3 oz. (4 cl) white tequila*
*1/3 oz. (1 cl) orange liqueur (such as Cointreau)*
*1/3 oz. (1 cl) banana liqueur (Crème de Bananes)*
*1 1/3 oz. (4 cl) orange juice*
*1 1/3 oz. (4 cl) banana nectar*
*2/3 oz. (2 cl) pineapple juice*
Plus:
*Ice cubes, shaker, bar strainer, tall glass (8 oz. / 24 cl), two drinking straws*

**1** Combine all ingredients into the shaker with four ice cubes. Cap the shaker and shake vigorously for 15 seconds.

**2** Pour the contents of the shaker through the bar strainer and into the glass over two or three more ice cubes. Serve with the drinking straws.

## After-dinner Drink **Apollo 8**
*(right in photo)*

Ingredients for one drink:
*2/3 oz. (2 cl) white tequila*
*2/3 oz. (2 cl) Blue Curaçao*
*1/3 oz. (1 cl) Galliano (Italian herb and spice liqueur)*
*2 oz. (6 cl) cream*
Plus:
*Ice cubes, shaker, bar strainer, cocktail glass (4 oz. / 12 cl)*

**1** Put all ingredients into the shaker with four ice cubes. Cap the shaker and shake vigorously for about 15 seconds.

**2** Pour the contents of the shaker through the bar strainer and into the glass.

## Sweet Drink **Green Poison**
*(center in photo)*

Ingredients for one drink:
*1 1/3 oz. (4 cl) white tequila*
*2/3 oz. (2 cl) Blue Curaçao*
*3 1/3 oz. (10 cl) peach nectar*
*2/3 oz. (2 cl) freshly squeezed lemon juice*
*2/3 oz. (2 cl) coconut syrup*
Plus:
*Ice cubes, shaker, bar strainer, large cocktail glass (10 oz. / 30 cl)*

**1** Put all ingredients into the shaker with four ice cubes. Cap the shaker and shake vigorously for about 15 seconds.

**2** Put two or three ice cubes into the glass. Pour the contents of the shaker over them through the bar strainer.

## Variation:
Instead of coconut syrup, try **cream of coconut** from a can. Then in a blender mix the ingredients with two or three Tbsp. of crushed ice.

## Garnish:
For this tropical flavored drink decorate the rim with shredded coconut. Before preparing the drink, run a quarter lemon around the rim of a cocktail glass and dip the glass in a dish filled with shredded coconut. Tap the glass gently to remove excess shredded coconut. Also, garnish with a slice of peach on the rim of the glass. Serve the drink with an orange-colored straw.

### Creamy Sweet Drink **Swimming Pool**

Ingredients for one drink:
**1 2/3 oz. (5 cl) vodka**
**3 1/3 oz. (10 cl) pineapple juice**
**2 Tbsp. sweet cream**
**2 tsp. cream of coconut (canned)**
**1/3 oz. (1 cl) Blue Curaçao**
Plus:
**Blender, crushed ice, large cocktail glass**
**(10 oz. / 30 cl)**

**1** Combine all ingredients except the Blue Curaçao into the blender. Blend thoroughly until foam appears.

**2** Fill the glass about half-full with crushed ice. Pour the blended mixture over the ice and stir well. Pour the Blue Curaçao over the prepared drink.

## Variation:

If you have **white rum** in the house, try the Swimming Pool with 1 oz. (3 cl) of white rum and 2/3 oz. (2 cl) of vodka instead of using 1 2/3 oz. (5 cl) of vodka.

## Nonalcoholic Variation:

To enjoy a Swimming Pool with **no alcohol**: Put 2/3 oz. (2 cl) Curaçao blue syrup, 2 tsp. cream of coconut (canned), 2/3 oz. (2 cl) heavy cream and 4 oz. (12 cl) of pineapple juice into the blender and blend. Put two or three ice cubes into a tall glass (8 oz. / 24 cl) and pour the blended mixture over them. Serve with a drinking straw.

## Fruity Drink **Apricot Touch**

Ingredients for one drink:
*1 1/3 oz. (4 cl) vodka*
*2/3 oz. (2 cl) apricot brandy*
*4 oz. (12 cl) apricot nectar*
*2/3 oz. (2 cl) Rose's lime juice*
*2/3 oz. (2 cl) grenadine syrup*
Plus:
*Ice cubes, shaker, bar strainer, tall glass*
*(10 oz. / 30 cl)*

**1** Combine all ingredients into the shaker. Cap
and shake vigorously for about 15 seconds.

**2** Put two or three ice cubes into the glass.
Pour the contents of the shaker through the
bar strainer and over the ice cubes.

## Party Drink **Sex on the Beach**

Ingredients for one drink:
*1 oz. (3 cl) vodka*
*1 oz. (3 cl) apricot brandy*
*2 oz. (6 cl) pineapple juice*
*1 oz. (3 cl) orange juice*
*1 oz. (3 cl) cherry juice*
Plus:
*Ice cubes, shaker, bar strainer, old-fashioned*
*glass (8 oz. / 24 cl)*

**1** Combine all ingredients into the shaker with
four ice cubes. Cap the shaker and shake vigorously for 15 seconds.

**2** Put two or three ice cubes in the glass.
Pour the contents of the shaker through the
bar strainer and over the ice cubes.

## Party Drink **Caipirovka**
*(right in photo)*

Ingredients for one drink:
*1 lime*
*2 oz. (6 cl) vodka*
*2 tsp. granulated sugar or 2/3 oz. (2 cl)*
*  cane syrup*
Plus:
*Ice cubes, pestle, old-fashioned glass*
*(5 oz. / 15 cl), two short drinking straws*

**1** Wash the lime in hot water, pat dry, and quarter it. Squeeze the juice into the glass and place the lime pieces into the glass with the juice.

**2** Use the pestle to crush the pieces of lime in the glass. Add a couple of ice cubes.

**3** Put the vodka and the sugar or cane syrup into the glass and stir. Put the straws into the glass.

## Creamy Drink **White Cloud**
*(left in photo)*

Ingredients for one drink:
*1 1/3 oz. (4 cl) vodka*
*2/3 oz. (2 cl) white cocoa liqueur (white crème*
*  de cacao)*
*2 oz. (6 cl) pineapple juice*
*2 Tbsp. heavy cream*
Plus:
*Ice cubes, crushed ice, shaker, bar strainer,*
*tall glass (8 oz. / 24 cl), drinking straw*

**1** Combine all ingredients into the shaker with four ice cubes. Cap the shaker and shake vigorously for about 15 seconds.

**2** Fill the glass about one-third full with crushed ice. Pour the contents of the shaker through the bar strainer over the ice. Serve with the drinking straw.

## Fruity Drink **Pretty in Pink**
*(center in photo)*

Ingredients for one drink:
*1 1/3 oz. (4 cl) vodka*
*3 1/3 oz. (10 cl) black currant nectar*
*1 1/3 oz. (4 cl) pink grapefruit juice*
*2/3 oz. (2 cl) Rose's lime juice*
Plus:
*Ice cubes, shaker, bar strainer, large cocktail*
*glass (10 oz. / 30 cl)*

**1** Combine all ingredients into the shaker with four ice cubes. Cap the shaker and shake vigorously for about 15 seconds.

**2** Put three or four ice cubes into the glass and pour the contents of the shaker through the strainer over the ice.

---

## *Cocktail Snack*

71

### *Trout Pockets*

Makes 20 pieces
Thaw 5 square slices of frozen puff pastry. Preheat the oven to 400°F (200°C). Cut the slices of pastry dough diagonally. Separate them to form four triangles. Brush the triangles with one whisked egg yolk. Sprinkle with a little salt. Reduce heat to 350°F (180°C) and bake in the oven (middle rack) for 10 minutes. In the meantime, puree 4 1/2 oz. (125 g) smoked trout filets with 2 Tbsp. of crème fraîche, 1–2 Tbsp. of finely chopped parsley, 2 tsp. of capers, the juice from half a lemon, and ground pepper. Remove the pastry dough from the oven. With a knife, cut the triangles diagonally and stuff them with the trout mousse.

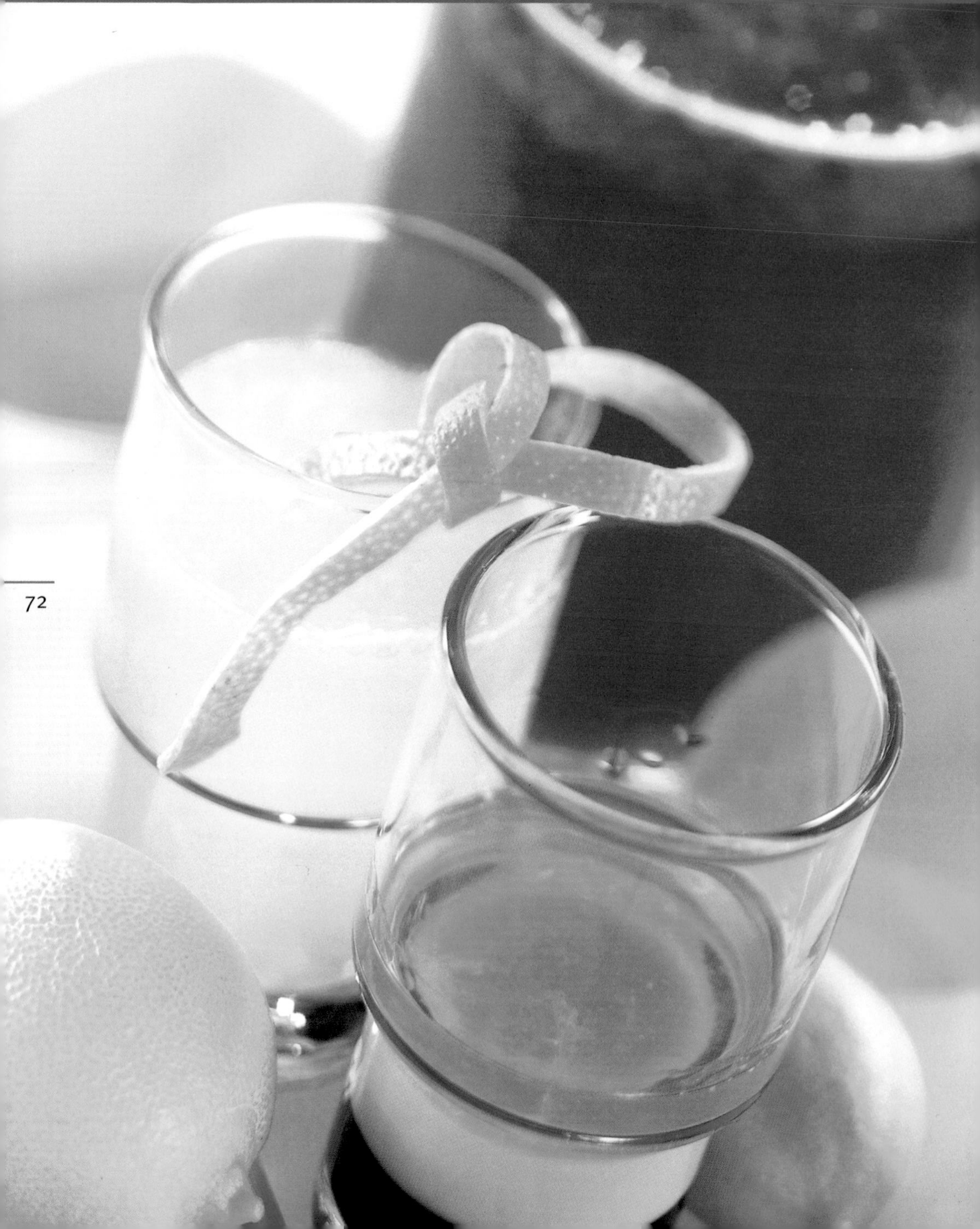

## Party Drink **Kamikaze**
*(center in photo)*

Ingredients for one drink:
**1 oz. (3 cl) ice-cold vodka**
**1/3 oz. (1 cl) bitter orange liqueur (Curaçao Triple Sec)**
**1/3 oz. (1 cl) freshly squeezed lemon juice**
**1/3 oz. (1 cl) Rose's lime juice**
Plus:
**Blender, old-fashioned glass (2 2/3 oz. / 8 cl)**

**1** Combine the vodka, bitter orange liqueur, lemon juice, and lime juice in the blender. Blend for about 20 seconds.

**2** Pour the blended mixture into the glass and serve immediately.

## Strong Drink **B 52**
*(front in photo)*

Ingredients for one drink:
**1/3 oz. (1 cl) coffee liqueur**
**1/3 oz. (1 cl) Irish cream liqueur (such as Bailey's)**
**1/3 oz. (1 cl) orange liqueur (such as Grand Marnier)**
Plus:
**Shot glass (1 1/3 oz. / 4 cl), short drinking straw**

**1** Here be careful. In the stated sequence pour the ingredients into the glass by letting the liqueurs run over the curved side of a teaspoon into the glass.

**2** With a cigarette lighter, light the B 52. Before drinking blow out the fire. Then drink through the straw.

## Party Drink **Berry Limes**
*(rear in photo)*

Ingredients for one drink:
**18 ounces (500 g) mixed frozen berries (raspberries, strawberries, black currants)**
**8 1/2 oz. (250 ml) vodka**
**2/3 oz. (20 ml) Rose's lime juice or freshly squeezed lime juice**
**3 1/2 oz. (100 ml) sparkling wine**
**Two or three Tbsp. sugar**
Plus:
**Blender, pitcher**

**1** Let the frozen berries thaw in a strainer. Blend the thawed berries to a smooth puree.

**2** Pour the vodka, lime juice, and sparkling wine over the berries. Mix briefly and add the sugar according to taste. Pour into a bottle or pitcher and keep cold until serving.

## Variation:
For a single drink: Thaw 5 frozen strawberries and put them in the blender along with 1 2/3 oz. (5 cl) vodka, 1 2/3 oz. (5 cl) bitter lemon, 2/3 oz. (2 cl) Rose's lime juice, and 2/3 oz. (2 cl) strawberry syrup. Blend to a smooth texture. Pour into a tall glass (8 oz. / 24 cl) and serve with two drinking straws.

## Substitutions:
Experiment with this drink! Match flavor to taste, mood, and season. Use **assorted berries** by themselves or blend using **kiwi fruit**, **melon**, and similar fruits.

# Low-Alcohol Drinks

# Quick to Make and Less Is More

*Down with the prejudice that less alcohol means less taste! Use low-alcohol drinks with aromatic high-proof spirits such as Cachaça. Or use ice cream or pureed fruits for an intense taste experience. You'll save time, too, especially with the quick-to-prepare drinks on this page:*

### Pineapple Batida
For 1 drink: Put 1 1/3 oz. (4 cl) coconut liqueux into a tall glass (8 oz. / 20 cl) along with two or three ice cubes. Top off with ice-cold pineapple juice.

### Campari Passion Fruit
For one drink: Put 1 1/3 oz. (4 cl) Campari into a tall glass (8 oz. / 24 cl) along with two or three ice cubes. Pour in ice-cold passion fruit nectar.

### Noble Beer
For one drink: Combine 1 oz. (3 cl) ice-cold light beer and 1 oz. (3 cl) ice-cold dry sparkling wine in a wineglass (3 1/3 oz. / 10 cl). Pour in ice-cold orange juice and stir briefly.

### Gin and Tonic
For one drink: Put 1 1/3 oz. (4 cl) gin into a tall glass (8 oz. / 24 cl) along with two or three ice cubes and half a lemon slice. Pour in ice-cold tonic water.

### Vodka Lemon
For one drink: Pour 1 1/3 oz. (4 cl) vodka into a tall glass (8 oz. / 24 cl) along with two or three ice cubes and half a lemon slice. Pour in ice-cold bitter lemon.

*Further quick drinks in this chapter include the following:*
Bordeaux Cobbler (p. 99)
Bull's Eye (p. 83)
C-O-L-L-ision (p. 79)
Florida (p. 79)
Fuzzy Navel (p. 91)
Pear Blues (p. 95)
Sherry Shandy (p. 97)
South Seas (p. 89)
Tomato Cocktail (p. 77)
Woody Woodpecker (p. 80)

*Other low-alcohol drinks in this book include the following:*
Bellini (p. 27)
Champagne Cocktail (p. 27)
Cuba Libre (p. 39; with 1 1/3 oz. / 4 cl rum)
Kir Royale (p. 27)
Pretty in Pink (p. 71)
Pretty Woman (p. 29)
Tequila Sunrise (p. 41; with 1 1/3 oz. / 4 cl) tequila and 4 oz. / 12 cl orange juice)

## Anise Blanc
Creamy Drink
*(left in photo)*

Ingredients for one drink:
**1 1/3 oz. (4 cl) anisette (Pernod or Ricard)**
**1 1/3 oz. (4 cl) orange juice**
**2/3 oz. (2 cl) almond syrup (orgeat)**
**1 2/3 oz. (5 cl) heavy cream**
Garnish:
**Shaved chocolate**
Plus:
**Ice cubes, shaker, bar strainer, tall glass**
**(8 oz. / 24 cl)**

**1** Combine all ingredients into the shaker with four ice cubes. Cap the shaker and shake vigorously for about 15 seconds.

**2** Pour the contents of the shaker through the bar strainer into the glass over three or four ice cubes. Top off the drink by sprinkling flakes of shaved chocolate.

## Tomato Cocktail
Classic Drink
*(center in photo)*

Ingredients for one drink:
**1 1/3 oz. (4 cl) anisette (Pernod or Ricard)**
**1/3 oz. (1 cl) grenadine syrup**
**Cold, plain mineral or spring water to top off**
Plus:
**Ice cubes, tall glass (8 oz. / 24 cl)**

**1** Into the tall glass combine the Pernod and the grenadine syrup with two or three ice cubes. Fill with cold mineral or spring water and stir well.

## Substitutions:
Instead of using water you can also use ginger ale. Then serve an **Anise Pink**.

## Crocodile
Fruity Drink
*(right in photo)*

Ingredients for one drink:
**2/3 oz. (2 cl) anisette (Pernod or Ricard)**
**2/3 oz. (2 cl) Blue Curaçao**
**1 dash angostura**
**2 oz. (6 cl) passion fruit nectar**
**2 oz. (6 cl) peach nectar**
Garnish:
**1/4 lemon, granulated sugar in a dish,**
**1 lemon slice**
Plus:
**Ice cubes, shaker, bar strainer, tall glass**
**(8 oz. / 24 cl), two drinking straws**

**1** Run the lemon quarter around the rim of the glass and dip the rim into a dish filled with sugar. Tap lightly on the glass to remove excess sugar.

**2** Combine all ingredients into the shaker with four ice cubes. Cap the shaker and shake vigorously for about 15 seconds. Pour the mixed drink through the bar strainer and into the glass over two or three ice cubes.

**3** Cut the lemon slice into the middle and hang it on the rim of the glass. Serve the drink with the straws.

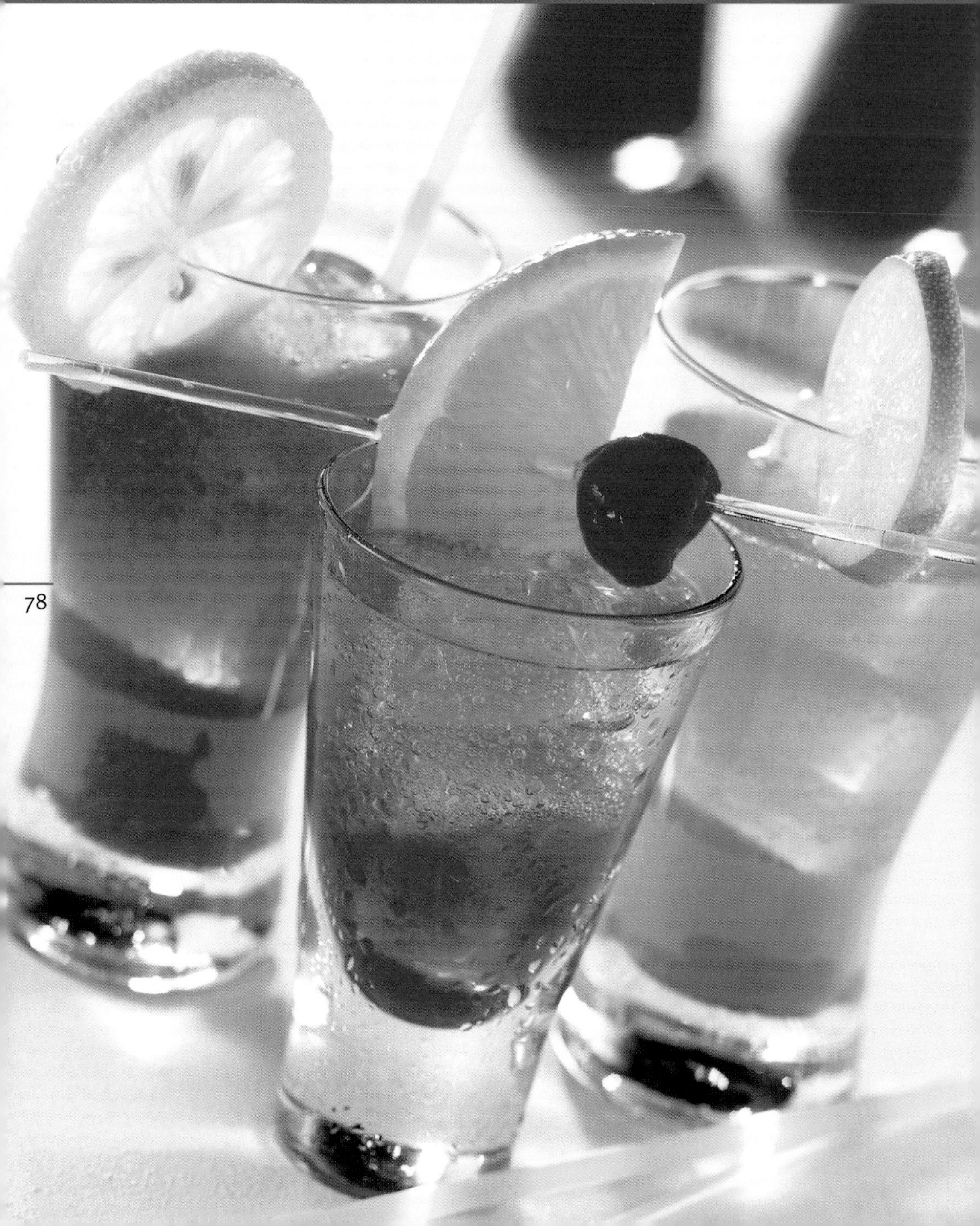

## Fruity Drink **Florida**
*(left in photo)*

Ingredients for one drink:
*1 1/3 oz. (4 cl) aperol*
*1 1/3 oz. (4 cl) grapefruit juice*
*Ice-cold tonic water*
Garnish:
*1 lemon slice*
Plus:
*Ice cubes, tall glass (8 oz. / 24 cl),
drinking straw*

**1** Put two or three ice cubes into the glass. Pour the aperol and grapefruit juice over them. Fill the glass with tonic water and stir gently.

**2** Cut the lemon slice across the middle and put it onto the rim of the glass. Serve with the straw.

## Aperitif **C-O-L-L-ision**
*(right in photo)*

Ingredients for one drink:
*2/3 oz. (2 cl) Campari*
*1 1/3 oz. (4 cl) orange juice*
*2/3 oz. (2 cl) freshly squeezed lime juice*
*2/3 oz. (2 cl) Rose's lime juice*
*Ice-cold tonic water*
Garnish:
*1/2 lime slice*
Plus:
*Ice cubes, tall glass (8 oz. / 24 cl)*

**1** Combine all ingredients except the tonic water into the glass with two or three ice cubes. Stir thoroughly.

**2** Top off with tonic water and once again stir briefly. Cut the lime slice across the middle and put it onto the rim of the glass.

## Substitutions:
If you want an even fruitier and tangier drink, replace the orange juice with **grapefruit juice**.

## Refreshing Drink **Aperol Sour**
*(center in photo)*

Ingredients for one drink:
*2 oz. (6 cl) aperol*
*1 1/3 oz. (4 cl) freshly squeezed lemon juice*
*1/3 oz. cane syrup*
Garnish:
*1/2 orange slice, 1 cocktail cherry, cocktail spear*
Plus:
*Ice cubes, shaker, bar strainer, old-fashioned glass (5 oz. / 15 cl)*

**1** Combine all ingredients into the shaker with four ice cubes. Cap the shaker and shake vigorously for about 15 seconds. Pour the drink through the bar strainer into the glass over two or three ice cubes.

**2** Spear the orange slice and the cocktail cherry and lay them across the rim of the glass.

## *Cocktail Snack*

### *Fig Morsels*

Makes 40 pieces
Carefully wipe 10 large figs with a clean kitchen towel and quarter them. Take 4 thin slices of Parma prosciutto (ham) and cut them into 40 shorter pieces. Wrap each fig piece in prosciutto. Mix and season about 4 thin slices (75 g) of Mascarpone cheese with salt, black pepper, and a little grated lemon peel. Put the mixture into a pastry bag with a star-shaped nozzle and squeeze it onto the figs. You could also garnish each slice of cheese with a pistachio nut.

### Tall Drink **Woody Woodpecker**

Ingredients for one drink:
*1 1/3 oz. (4 cl) Cachaça*
*5 oz. (15 cl) orange juice*
*1/3 oz. (1 cl) Galliano (Italian herb and spice liqueur)*
Plus:
*Ice cubes, large cocktail glass (10 oz. / 30 cl)*

**1** Put three or four ice cubes into the glass. Pour the Cachaça and orange juice over them and stir.

**2** Add the Galliano over the drink and serve immediately.

## Substitutions:

No Galliano in the house? Just leave it out and increase the amount of Cachaça by 1 2/3 oz. (5 cl).

80

### Tall Drink **Brasilic Ale**

Ingredients for one drink:
*1 lime*
*1 1/3 oz. (4 cl) Cachaça*
*Ginger ale to top off*
Plus:
*Crushed ice, tall glass (8 oz. / 24 cl), drinking straw*

**1** Wash the lime in hot water, pat it dry, and cut it into eighths. Squeeze the juice into the tall glass and add the lime pieces into the glass.

**2** Fill the glass about half-full with crushed ice. Pour the Cachaça over it. Top off with ginger ale and stir gently. Serve with the drinking straw.

Tropical Drink **Batida de Banana**

Ingredients for one drink:
*1/2 soft , ripe banana*
*1 dash freshly squeezed lemon juice*
*1 1/3 oz. (4 cl) Cachaça*
*2 2/3 oz. (8 cl) pineapple juice*
*2/3 oz. (2 cl) banana nectar*
*1/3 oz. (1 cl) cane syrup*
Plus:
*Ice cubes, crushed ice, blender, tall glass*
*(8 oz. / 24 cl)*

**1** Puree the banana halves along with the lemon juice in the blender.

**2** Add and blend well the Cachaça, pineapple juice, banana nectar, cane syrup, and two Tbsp. of crushed ice. Pour the mixture into the glass over two or three more ice cubes.

## Substitutions:
Use 2 oz. (6 cl) of passion fruit nectar instead of the pineapple juice and the banana nectar. Then, instead of using the banana puree, wash one lime in hot water and quarter it. Squeeze the juice into the glass and put the lime pieces into the glass. Use a pestle to squeeze out the lime juice again. Add a couple of ice cubes and pour in the Cachaça, passion fruit nectar, and 2/3 oz. (2 cl) of cane syrup. Stir well, and you have the **Batida de Maracuja con Limao**!

## Garnish:
To make it taste twice as good: On a cocktail spear skewer alternating **slices of banana** (first soaked briefly in lemon juice) and **chunks of pineapple**. Place the skewer on the rim of the glass.

## Tall Drink **Bull's Eye**
*(right in photo)*

Ingredients for one drink:
*1 oz. (3 cl) cognac or brandy*
*2 oz. (6 cl) apple juice*
*Ice-cold ginger ale to top off*
Garnish:
*1 sprig fresh mint*
Plus:
*Ice cubes, tall glass (8 oz. / 24 cl), drinking straw*

**1** Put two or three ice cubes into the glass. Pour the cognac first, then the apple juice over them. Stir well.

**2** Top off with ginger ale. Wash the sprig of mint, shake it dry, and put it into the drink. Serve with the drinking straw.

## Garnish:
In addition to—or instead of—the sprig of fresh mint, stick a spiral of apple peel on the rim of the glass.

## Fruit Drink **Fruity Brandy**
*(center in photo)*

Ingredients for one drink:
*1 1/3 oz. (4 cl) brandy*
*2 2/3 oz. (8 cl) pineapple juice*
*1 1/3 oz. (4 cl) apricot nectar*
*2/3 oz. (2 cl) banana nectar*
*1/3 oz. (1 cl) grenadine syrup*
Plus:
*Ice cubes, shaker, bar strainer, large cocktail glass (10 oz. / 30 cl)*

**1** Combine all ingredients along with four ice cubes into the shaker. Cap the shaker and shake vigorously for about 15 seconds.

**2** Put two or three ice cubes into the glass. Pour the contents of the shaker through the bar strainer over the ice cubes.

## Aromatic Drink **Matador**
*(left in photo)*

Ingredients for one drink:
*2/3 oz. (2 cl) cognac or brandy*
*2 2/3 oz. (8 cl) milk*
*1/3 oz. (1 cl) cane syrup (to taste)*
*Freshly grated nutmeg*
*Powdered cinnamon*
Plus:
*Ice cubes, shaker, bar strainer, cocktail glass (4 oz. / 12 cl)*

**1** Combine the cognac, milk, and cane syrup (to taste) into the shaker with four ice cubes. Cap the shaker and shake vigorously for about 15 seconds.

**2** Pour the contents of the shaker through the bar strainer into the glass.

**3** Sprinkle over the drink a little freshly grated nutmeg and powdered cinnamon. Serve immediately.

## Nonalcoholic Variation:
Making it easy without alcohol: Instead of cognac, use 2/3 oz. (2 cl) each of almond syrup (orgeat) and cream of coconut (canned). Increase the milk to 4 oz. (12 cl). Prepare the shaker with four ice cubes and shake as described above. Pour the contents of the shaker through the bar strainer and into a tall glass (8 oz. / 24 cl). Sprinkle the drink with freshly grated nutmeg.

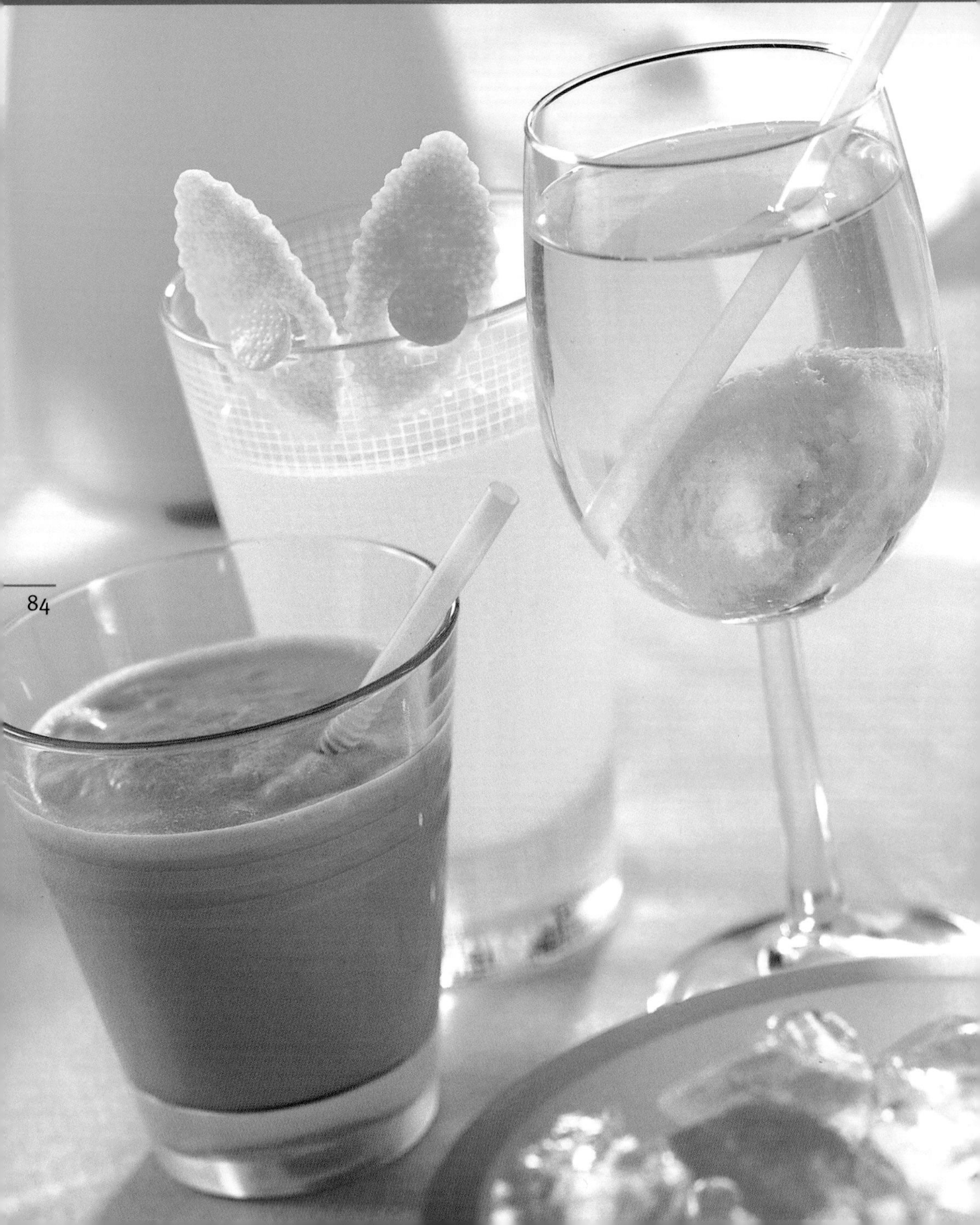

## Summer Drink **Happy Apricot**

*(right in photo)*

Ingredients for one drink:
*2 scoops vanilla ice cream*
*2/3 oz. (2 cl) apricot nectar*
*1 dash apricot brandy*
*Cold, dry white wine to top off*
Plus:
*Large cocktail or wineglass (10 oz. / 30 cl),*
*drinking straw*

**1** Put the vanilla ice cream into the cocktail or wineglass; pour the apricot nectar and apricot brandy over it.

**2** Slowly pour in the white wine and serve with the drinking straw.

## Tangy Drink **Bitter Swirl**

*(left in photo)*

Ingredients for one drink:
*2 scoops vanilla ice cream*
*2/3 oz. (2 cl) Campari*
*3 oz. (6 cl) clear lemonade*
Plus:
*Ice cubes, blender, tall glass (8 oz. / 24 cl),*
*drinking straw*

**1** Combine the vanilla ice cream in the blender with the Campari, lemonade, and one ice cube. Blend for about 30 seconds.

**2** Pour the mixture into the glass and serve with the straw.

## Nonalcoholic Variation:
For an alcohol-free and less tangy variation, instead of the Campari use **grenadine syrup**.

## Refreshing Drink **Frozen Vodka Lemon**

*(center in photo)*

Ingredients for one drink:
*2 scoops lemon sherbet*
*2/3 oz. (2 cl) vodka*
*6 2/3 oz. (20 cl) bitter lemon*
Plus:
*Ice cubes, blender, large cocktail glass*
*(10 oz. / 30 cl)*

**1** Put the lemon sherbet into the blender with the vodka, bitter lemon, and one ice cube. Blend for about 30 seconds.

**2** Pour the mixture into the glass and serve immediately.

## Substitutions:
The combination of ice cream, spirits, and lemonade or juice offers countless possible variations. One fine trio combines **orange sherbet**, **orange liqueur**, and dry **sparkling wine**. For a low-alcohol variation, instead of sparkling wine, use orange soda or orange juice. Another delicious and low-alcohol possibility: a mixture of **peach ice cream, orange liqueur,** and **pineapple juice.**

---

### Tall Drink **Bittersweet Symphony**

Ingredients for one drink:
*1 1/3 oz. (4 cl) coconut liqueur (such as Batida de Coco)*
*2 2/3 oz. (8 cl) grapefruit juice*
*1/3–2/3 oz. (1–2 cl) grenadine syrup*
Garnish:
*1 cocktail cherry*
Plus:
*Ice cubes, shaker, bar strainer, tall glass (8 oz. / 24 cl)*

**1** Combine all ingredients in the shaker with four ice cubes. Cap the shaker and shake vigorously for about 15 seconds.

**2** Pour the contents of the shaker through the bar strainer over two or three ice cubes in the glass. Serve with the cocktail cherry garnish.

### Refreshing Drink **Blue Hour**

Ingredients for one drink:
*1 1/3 oz. (4 cl) Blue Curaçao*
*2 2/3 oz. (8 cl) pineapple juice*
*2 2/3 oz. (8 cl) banana nectar*
Plus:
*Ice cubes, shaker, bar strainer, large cocktail glass (10 oz. / 30 cl)*

**1** Combine all the ingredients in the shaker with four ice cubes. Cap the shaker and shake vigorously for about 15 seconds.

**2** Pour the contents of the shaker through the bar strainer into the glass.

## Substitutions:

For a tangy flavor, mix this tall drink with **grapefruit juice** instead of using banana nectar.

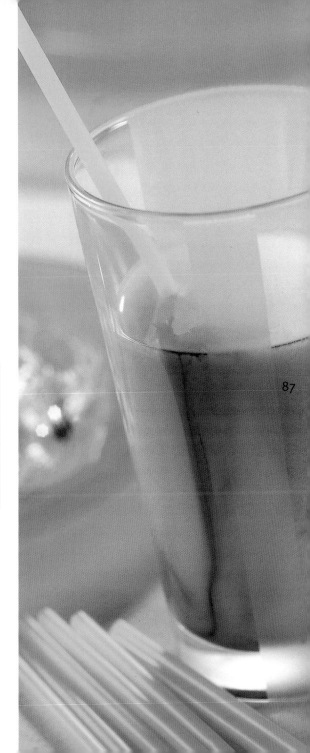

Tropical Drink **Coco Sunrise**

Ingredients for one drink:
*2 oz. (6 cl) coconut liqueur*
*3–4 oz. (10–12 cl) orange juice*
*1/3 oz. (1 cl) grenadine syrup*
Plus:
*Ice cubes, shaker, bar strainer, tall glass*
*(8 oz. / 24 cl), drinking straw*

**1** Put the coconut liqueur and the orange juice into the shaker with four ice cubes. Cap the shaker and shake vigorously for about 15 seconds. Pour the mixture through the strainer into the glass.

**2** Pour the grenadine syrup carefully over the drink. Serve with the drinking straw. Stir well before drinking.

## *Happy Hour*

In case you have a lot of people who want a Tropical Sunrise, leave the shaker in the cupboard and make the tall drink right in the glass. However, use slightly larger glasses (such as large cocktail glasses with a capacity of 10 oz. / 30 cl) to accommodate lots of ice cubes.

# Fuzzy Navel
(not pictured)

Ingredients for one drink:
*1 part peach schnapps*
*1 part orange juice*
*1 part lemonade*

**1** Mix equal parts of each ingredient in a tall glass (8 oz. / 24 cl), top with ice, garnish with an orange slice, and serve.

## Tall Drink **South Seas**
*(left in photo)*

Ingredients for one drink:
*1 oz. (3 cl) orange liqueur (such as Cointreau)*
*1/3 oz. (1 cl) Blue Curaçao*
*1 1/3 oz. pineapple juice*
*Ice-cold ginger ale to top off*
Plus:
*Ice cubes, tall glass (7 oz. / 20 cl), two drinking straws*

**1** Put two or three ice cubes into the glass. Pour all ingredients except the ginger ale over them. Stir thoroughly.

**2** Top off with ginger ale and serve with the drinking straws.

## Garnish:
For a tropical-style drink: Skewer one **cocktail cherry**, one **pineapple chunk**, and a couple of **pineapple leaves** on a cocktail spear and lay it across the rim of the glass.

## Sour Drink **Refreshing Cassis**
*(right in photo)*

Ingredients for one drink:
*1/3 oz. (1 cl) white rum*
*1 oz. (3 cl) black currant liqueur (cassis)*
*3 1/3 oz. (10 cl) orange juice*
*2/3 oz. (2 cl) freshly squeezed lime juice*
Plus:
*Ice cubes, shaker, bar strainer, tall glass (8 oz. / 24 cl)*

**1** Combine all ingredients in the shaker with four ice cubes. Cap the shaker and shake vigorously for about 15 seconds.

**2** Pour the contents of the shaker through the bar strainer over one or two ice cubes in the glass.

## Fruity Drink **Comfort Cooler**
*(center in photo)*

Ingredients for one drink:
*1 1/3 oz. (4 cl) Southern Comfort*
*4 oz. (12 cl) pineapple juice*
*2/3 oz. (2 cl) freshly squeezed lime juice*
Garnish:
*1 lime slice, 1 cocktail cherry, cocktail spear*
Plus:
*Ice cubes, shaker, bar strainer, large cocktail glass (10 oz. / 30 cl), two drinking straws*

**1** Combine all ingredients in the shaker with four ice cubes. Cap the shaker and shake vigorously for about 15 seconds. Pour the mixture through the bar strainer over four to six ice cubes in the glass.

**2** Cut the lime slice in the middle and stick it on a spear. Spear the cherry with the cocktail spear and place it on the glass rim. Serve the drink with the straws.

## *Cocktail Snack*

### *Guacamole*

Serves 4–6
Cut two ripe avocados in half and remove the seeds. Dig out the flesh with a spoon and puree it in the blender. Add the juice of half a lime and blend. Clean two or three scallions and mince them. Wash one or two tomatoes. Cut out the stem area and cube the flesh. Into the avocado puree, stir the onions and tomatoes. Season the guacamole with salt, black pepper, and powdered cumin. Serve with taco chips or crackers.

Mild Drink **Ireland Orange**

*(rear in photo)*

Ingredients for one drink:
*1 1/3 oz. (4 cl) Irish cream liqueur (such*
  *as Bailey's)*
*2/3 oz. (2 cl) almond liqueur (such as*
  *Amaretto)*
*Approx. 4 oz. (10–12 cl) orange juice*
Plus:
*Ice cubes, shaker, bar strainer, tall glass*
*(8 oz. / 24 cl)*

**1** Combine all ingredients into the shaker with
four ice cubes. Cap the shaker and shake vigorously for about 15 seconds.

**2** Pour the contents of the shaker through the
bar strainer into the glass.

Fruity Drink **Florida Comfort**

*(front in photo)*

Ingredients for one drink:
*1 1/3 oz. (4 cl) Southern Comfort*
*3 1/3 oz. (10 cl) orange juice*
*2/3 oz. (2 cl) freshly squeezed lemon juice*
*1/3–2/3 oz. (1–2 cl) grenadine syrup*
Plus:
*Ice cubes, shaker, bar strainer, tall glass*
*(8 oz. / 24 cl), two drinking straws*

**1** Combine all ingredients in the shaker with
four ice cubes. Cap the shaker and shake vigorously for about 15 seconds.

**2** Put one or two ice cubes into the glass. Pour
the contents of the shaker through the bar
strainer and over the ice. Serve the drink with
the two drinking straws.

Refreshing Drink **Turquoise**

*(center in photo)*

Ingredients for one drink:
*1/3 oz. (1 cl) white rum*
*1 1/3 oz. (4 cl) Blue Curaçao*
*2 oz. (6 cl) banana nectar*
*2/3 oz. (2 cl) Rose's lime juice*
*2 oz. (6 cl) buttermilk*
Plus:
*Ice cubes, shaker, bar strainer, tall glass*
*(8 oz. / 24 cl)*

**1** Combine all ingredients into the shaker with
four ice cubes. Cap the shaker and shake vigorously for about 15 seconds.

**2** Pour the contents of the shaker through the
bar strainer into the glass. A spear of banana
slices and pieces of orange (as picture) will be
beautiful and delicious with this turquoise-
colored buttermilk drink.

## Low-Alcohol Variation:

If you want a drink with even less alcohol, use
the same amount of **Curaçao Bleu syrup** instead
of the 1 1/3 oz. (4 cl) of Blue Curaçao.

## Garnish:

A spear of banana slices and pieces of orange
will be beautiful and delicious with the
turquoise-colored buttermilk drink. The taste
will be twice as good if the pieces of orange are
peeled. How to do it: Peel the orange right down
to the fruit making sure that the white skin
under the peel is also removed. Using a sharp
knife separate the wedges from the dividing
membrane. Depending on their size, cut them
into halves or thirds, and spear the pieces along
with the banana slices.

### Summer Drink Sweet Ruby

Ingredients for one drink:
**5 fresh, ripe strawberries**
**2/3 oz. (2 cl) aperol**
**1 oz. (3 cl) apricot nectar**
**1/3 oz. (1 cl) strawberry syrup**
**Ice-cold Prosecco to top off**
Plus:
**Ice cubes, blender, wineglass (8 oz. / 24 cl)**

**1** Wash the strawberries, pat them dry, and remove the stems. Put the strawberries into the blender and add the aperol, the apricot nectar, the strawberry syrup, a dash of Prosecco, and 1 ice cube. Mix thoroughly for 6 to 8 seconds or until the mixture is homogeneous.

**2** Pour the mixture into the wineglass; pour in the Prosecco, and stir briefly.

92

### Aperitif Kiwi's Fate

Ingredients for one drink:
**1 medium-size ripe kiwi**
**1/6 oz. (0.5 cl) Blue Curaçao**
**1/3 oz. (1 cl) banana syrup**
**Ice-cold Prosecco to top off**
Plus:
**Crushed ice, blender, wineglass (3 1/3 oz. / 10 cl)**

**1** Peel the kiwi and remove the seeds. Cut the fruit into large cubes. Combine the kiwi pieces, the banana syrup, and the Blue Curaçao in the blender together with 1 dash of Prosecco and two Tbsp. of crushed ice. Mix for 6 to 8 seconds or until the mixture is homogeneous.

**2** Pour the mixture into the wineglass and top off with Prosecco. Stir briefly and serve immediately.

**Sparkling Passion Fruit**

Ingredients for one drink:
*1 1/3 oz. (4 cl) passion fruit nectar*
*2/3 oz. (2 cl) orange juice*
*1 dash freshly squeezed lemon juice*
*1/3 oz. (1 cl) grenadine syrup*
*Ice-cold Prosecco to top off*
Plus:
*Ice cubes, shaker, bar strainer, wineglass*
*(8 oz. / 24 cl)*

**1** Combine all ingredients except the Prosecco
into the shaker with four ice cubes. Cap the
shaker and shake vigorously for about
15 seconds.

**2** Pour the contents of the shaker through the
bar strainer into the wineglass. Gently top off
with Prosecco.

## *Cocktail Snack*

### *Cheese and Crackers*

Makes 20
Clean, wash, and mince two scallions. Mix
a medium-sized block of soft goat cheese
about 7–8 oz. (200 g) with the scallions and
1/2 tsp. powdered cumin, and 1/4 tsp. chili
powder. Moisten your hands before forming
small balls of the cheese mixture. Wash one
bundle of mint and shake it dry. Pluck off the
leaves and mince them. Roll the cheese balls
in the minced mint. Refrigerate for an hour.
Cut the cheeseballs in half and put each half
on a cracker.

93

## Sweet Drink **Red Kiss**
*(right in photo)*

Ingredients for one drink:
*2 2/3 oz. (8 cl) sour cherry nectar*
*1 1/3 oz. (4 cl) coconut syrup*
*Ice-cold Prosecco to top off*
Plus:
*Ice cubes, shaker, bar strainer, wineglass*
*(8 oz. / 24 cl)*

**1** Combine the coconut syrup and the sour cherry juice in the shaker with four ice cubes. Cap the shaker and shake vigorously for about 15 seconds.

**2** Pour the contents of the shaker through the bar strainer into the wineglass. Top off with Prosecco and serve immediately.

## Tall Drink **Pear Blue**
*(center in photo)*

Ingredients for one drink:
*2/3 oz. (2 cl) Blue Curaçao*
*2 2/3 oz. (8 cl) pear juice*
*Ice-cold Prosecco to top off*
Plus:
*Ice cubes, tall glass (8 oz. / 24 cl)*

**1** Put two or three ice cubes into the glass. Pour the Blue Curaçao and the pear juice over them and stir well.

**2** Carefully top off with Prosecco and serve immediately.

## Garnish:
For a visual treat, hang a wedge of pear on the rim of the glass or put it right into the drink.

## Aperitif **Dream of Peach**
*(left in photo)*

Ingredients for one drink:
*1 1/3 oz. (4 cl) peach nectar*
*2/3 oz. (2 cl) apricot nectar*
*1/3 oz. (1 cl) grenadine syrup*
*Ice-cold Prosecco to top off*
Plus:
*Ice cubes, shaker, bar strainer, short old-fashioned glass (3 1/3 oz. / 10 cl)*

**1** Combine the peach nectar, the apricot nectar, and the grenadine syrup in the shaker with four ice cubes. Cap the shaker and shake vigorously for about 15 seconds.

**2** Pour the contents of the shaker through the bar strainer into the glass. Gently top off with Prosecco and serve immediately.

## *Cocktail Snack*

### *Baked Munchies*

Makes 20 pieces
Next to one another, lay out 4 square slices of frozen philo dough (10.5 oz / 300 g) and let thaw. Preheat oven to 400°F (200°C). With a fork, poke each slice of dough several times. Cut each slice into five strips 1 inch (2 cm) wide. Whisk two egg yolks and brush the liquid over the dough strips. Season the dough strips with salt and pepper; sprinkle some strips with sesame seeds and some strips with poppy seeds. Twist the strips into spirals and brush more egg yolk over the uncoated parts. Place the spirals on a baking sheet covered with baking paper. Reduce oven heat to 350°F (180°C) and bake on the middle rack for 15–20 minutes.

Tart Drink **Summery Sherry**

Ingredients for one drink:
**1 1/3 oz. (4 cl) medium sherry**
**2 oz. (6 cl) each apricot nectar and orange juice**
**2/3 oz. (2 cl) freshly squeezed lime juice**
**1/3 to 2/3 oz. (1–2 cl) cane syrup**
Garnish:
**1 orange peel**
Plus:
**Ice cubes, shaker, bar strainer, large cocktail glass (10 oz. / 30 cl), two drinking straws**

**1** Combine all ingredients in the shaker with four ice cubes. Cap the shaker and shake vigorously for about 15 seconds.

**2** Pour the contents of the shaker through the bar strainer over three or four ice cubes in the glass. Cut the orange slice in the middle and hang it on the rim of the glass. Serve with the drinking straws.

Creamy Drink **Spanish Cream**

Ingredients for one drink:
**1 1/3 oz. (4 cl) medium sherry**
**1/3 oz. (1 cl) brandy**
**1 1/3 oz. (4 cl) orange juice**
**1 1/3 oz. (4 cl) heavy cream**
**1/3 oz. (1 cl) cane syrup**
Garnish:
**Finely chopped pistachio nuts**
Plus:
**Ice cubes, shaker, bar strainer, old-fashioned glass (5 oz. / 15 cl)**

**1** Combine all ingredients in the shaker with four ice cubes. Cap the shaker and shake vigorously for about 15 seconds.

**2** Pour the contents of the shaker through the bar strainer over one or two ice cubes in the glass. Sprinkle the drink with the chopped pistachios.

Refreshing Drink **Sherry Shandy**

Ingredients for one drink:
**3 dashes angostura**
**1 1/3 oz. (4 cl) medium sherry**
**Ice-cold ginger ale to top off**
Plus:
**Ice cubes, tall glass (8 oz. / 24 cl)**

**1** Pour the angostura into the glass. Swirl the glass around so that the entire inside of the glass is coated with the liquid.

**2** Pour the sherry into the prepared glass and top off with ginger ale. Add one or two ice cubes to the drink and serve immediately.

## *Cocktail Snack*

### *Feta Pockets*

Makes 8 pockets
Thaw 12 oz. (300 g) of frozen spinach and 12 oz. (300 g) of frozen puff pastry dough (4 sheets) and slice them. Peel two cloves of garlic. Crumble 3/4–1 cup sheep's milk cheese (feta). Wash and chop fine one bunch of parsley. Preheat the oven to 400°F (200°C). Squeeze out the thawed spinach and chop coarsely. Add and stir in the garlic, the feta cheese, the parsley, 2 small eggs, and 2 Tbsp. of sour cream. Season with a little salt, pepper, and 1/2 tsp. powdered cumin. On a floured surface, roll out the sheets of dough to twice their size and cut them in half. Put the spinach mixture on one side of the dough and fold them over. Press together the edges of the dough. Place the stuffed pockets on a baking sheet lined with baking paper. Brush the pockets with a mixture of egg yolk and one Tbsp. milk. Reduce heat to 350°F (180°C). Bake on the middle rack of the oven for about 25 minutes.

## Party Drink **Swinging Girl**
*(right in photo)*

Ingredients for one drink:
*1/3 oz. (1 cl) gin*
*1 1/3 oz. (4 cl) dry white wine*
*1 dash Blue Curaçao*
*1/3 oz. (1 cl) mango nectar*
*Ice-cold ginger ale to top off*
Garnish:
*Slice of mango*
Plus:
*Ice cubes, shaker, bar strainer, tall glass
(8 oz. / 24 cl), drinking straw*

**1** Combine all ingredients except for the ginger ale in the shaker with four ice cubes. Cap the shaker and shake vigorously for about 15 seconds.

**2** Pour the contents of the shaker through the bar strainer over two or three ice cubes in the glass. Top off with the ginger ale and serve with the straw.

## Aperitif **East-West Connection**
*(left in photo)*

Ingredients for one drink:
*1 1/3 oz. (4 cl) sake (Japanese rice wine; available in Asian food stores)*
*2/3 oz. (2 cl) Campari*
*2 oz. (6 cl) pink grapefruit juice*
*1 1/3 oz. (4 cl) orange juice*
Plus:
*Ice cubes, shaker, bar strainer, tall glass
(8 oz. / 24 cl)*

**1** Combine the sake, the Campari, the grapefruit and orange juices in the shaker with four ice cubes. Cap the shaker and shake vigorously for about 15 seconds.

**2** Put two or three ice cubes into the glass. Pour the contents of the shaker through the bar strainer over the ice.

## Refreshing Drink **Bordeaux Cobbler**
*(center in photo)*

Ingredients for one drink:
*1 tsp. confectioner's sugar*
*2 tsp. club soda or mineral water*
*3 1/3 oz. (10 cl) Bordeaux or other French country wine*
Plus:
*Crushed ice, wineglass (8 oz. / 24 cl), drinking straw*

**1** Put the confectioner's sugar into the wineglass and add the club soda or mineral water. Stir until the sugar is dissolved.

**2** Add the red wine and fill the glass with enough crushed ice to form a little hump on top. Serve with the straw.

## *Happy Hour*

Want to treat your guests to a wine mixture? Make Spanish **sangria**! It's a little more work, but it can be prepared ahead of time. Serves 6–8: Peel, core, quarter, and slice three apples. Wash three oranges in hot water, dry them, and cut them into slices. Quarter the orange slices. Sprinkle the fruits with sugar. Let steep in 1 2/3 oz. (5 cl) each of orange liqueur and brandy for at least 30 minutes with one cinnamon stick. Pour over two bottles of Spanish red wine and refrigerate. Before serving add two lemons cut into slices and lots of ice cubes.

# The Harmony of Juices

*Sensible reasons to do without alcohol—anxiety over losing your driver's license, fear of hangover the morning after, etc. Alcohol-free cocktails are in no way inferior to their stronger relatives—as long as they are made properly. Here's what's involved:*

## Quality Is First Priority!

Mixing without alcohol means, above all, using fruit juices. In this case, keep in mind that it is not only mixture combinations, but quality of ingredients that determines the taste! It's always worth reading the labels when shopping. Fruit juices are really only the drinks that consist of 100 percent squeezed fruit and contain no water and/or added sugars. There is a distinction between natural fruit juice, that is, freshly harvested and squeezed and immediately packaged, and fruit juice from concentrate, which must be so labeled. Both are good candidates for mixed drinks, and shouldn't be replaced by nectars. Exceptions include black currant and passion fruit nectars; in undiluted form the juices from black currants and passion fruit are unpalatable, so they are turned into nectars, that is, they are mixed with sugar and water.

## Which with What?

There are essentially no limits to creativity with alcohol-free drinks; however, to monitor taste, there is one rule of thumb: Don't use only sweet or only tangy juices, but rather use balanced combinations of both. Here are a few suggestions for your own attempts at mixing:

**Pineapple Juice**
+ orange juice + passion fruit juice

**Apple Juice**
+ pear juice + ginger ale

**Apricot Nectar**
+ orange juice + lemon juice

**Banana Nectar**
+ orange juice + lemon juice + grenadine syrup

**Grapefruit Juice**
+ apple juice + pineapple juice + lime juice

**Cherry Juice**
+ pineapple juice + Rose's lime juice

**Orange Juice**
+ grapefruit juice + grenadine syrup + heavy cream

**Orange Juice**
+ passion fruit nectar + cream

**Orange Juice**
+ pineapple juice + cream of coconut + grenadine syrup

**Peach Nectar**
+ orange juice + lemon juice

## Classic Drink **Alice**

*(left in photo)*

Ingredients for one drink:
*2 2/3 oz. (8 cl) orange juice*
*2 2/3 oz. (8 cl) pineapple juice*
*2/3 oz. (2 cl) grenadine syrup*
*2/3 oz. (2 cl) heavy cream*
Plus:
*Ice cubes, shaker, bar strainer, large cocktail glass (10 oz. / 30 cl), two drinking straws*

1 Combine all ingredients in the shaker with four ice cubes. Cap the shaker and shake vigorously for about 15 seconds.

2 Pour the contents of the shaker through the bar strainer over three or four ice cubes in the glass. Serve with the straws.

## Fruit Drink **Car Driver**

*(right front in photo)*

Ingredients for one drink:
*3 1/3 oz. (10 cl) blood orange juice*
*2 oz. (6 cl) pineapple juice*
*2/3 oz. (2 cl) freshly squeezed lemon juice*
*2/3 oz. (2 cl) passion fruit syrup*
Garnish:
*1 lemon slice*
Plus:
*Ice cubes, shaker, bar strainer, large cocktail glass (10 oz. / 30 cl)*

1 Combine all ingredients except the lemon slice in the shaker with four ice cubes. Cap the shaker and shake vigorously for about 15 seconds.

2 Put two or three ice cubes into the glass and pour the contents of the shaker through the bar strainer over them. Cut the lemon slice across the middle and hang it on the rim of the glass.

## Creamy Drink **Cinderella**

*(photo rear middle)*

Ingredients for one drink:
*2 2/3 oz. (8 cl) grapefruit juice*
*2 2/3 oz. (8 cl) pineapple juice*
*2/3 oz. (2 cl) coconut syrup*
*1/3 oz. (1 cl) grenadine syrup*
*2/3 oz. (2 cl) heavy cream*
Plus:
*Ice cubes, shaker, bar strainer, large cocktail glass (10 oz. / 30 cl), drinking straw*

1 Combine all ingredients in the shaker with four ice cubes. Cap the shaker and shake vigorously for about 15 seconds.

2 Pour the contents of the shaker through the bar strainer over two or three ice cubes. Serve with the drinking straw.

## Garnish:

If you want your Cinderella to look nicer: Skewer two pineapple leaves on a cocktail spear and alternate cocktail cherries and banana slices (first drizzle the banana slices with lemon juice). Hang the fruit spear on the rim of the glass.

# Spring Awakening

*(left in photo)*

Ingredients for one drink:
*2 oz. (6 cl) blood orange juice*
*2/3 oz. (2 cl) pineapple juice*
*2/3 oz. (2 cl) passion fruit nectar*
*2/3 oz. (2 cl) cherry juice*
*2/3 oz. (2 cl) freshly squeezed lemon juice*
*2/3 oz. (2 cl) mango syrup*
Plus:
*Ice cubes, crushed ice, shaker, bar strainer, tall glass (8 oz. / 24 cl)*

**1** Combine all ingredients in the shaker with four ice cubes. Cap the shaker and shake vigorously for about 15 seconds.

**2** Fill the glass with crushed ice about a third full and pour the contents of the shaker through the bar strainer over the ice.

Creamy Drink # Tempting Orange

*(rear in photo)*

Ingredients for one drink:
*3 1/3 oz. (10 cl) orange juice*
*2 oz. (6 cl) passion fruit nectar*
*2 Tbsp. (2 cl) each almond syrup (orgeat) and heavy cream*
Garnish:
*1/4 lemon, finely chopped almonds (in a dish)*
Plus:
*Shaker, bar strainer, large cocktail glass (10 oz. / 30 cl), drinking straw*

**1** Run the lemon quarter around the rim of the glass and dip the glass into the dish with the chopped almonds. Tap the glass gently to remove excess almonds.

**2** Place all ingredients into the shaker with four ice cubes. Cap the shaker and shake vigorously for about 15 seconds.

**3** Put three or four ice cubes into the glass and pour the contents of the shaker through the bar strainer over them. Serve the drink with the drinking straw.

Tangy Drink # Dragon Heart

*(right in photo)*

Ingredients for one drink:
*4 oz. (12 cl) cherry juice*
*1 1/3 oz. (4 cl) passion fruit nectar*
*2/3 oz. (2 cl) freshly squeezed lemon juice*
*2/3 oz. (2 cl) grenadine syrup*
Plus:
*Ice cubes, shaker, bar strainer, large cocktail glass (10 oz. / 30 cl)*

**1** Combine all ingredients in the shaker with four ice cubes. Cap the shaker and shake vigorously for about 15 seconds.

**2** Put three or four ice cubes into the glass. Pour the contents of the shaker through the bar strainer over them.

# Cocktail Snack

## Cherry Muffins

Makes 12 muffins
In a strainer, drain 1/2 glass preserved cherries in their juice (approx. 1 1/2 cup / 175 g drained weight). Put a paper liner in each cup of the muffin tin. Preheat the oven to 400°F (200°C). Make a muffin batter by combining enough muffin mix with the cherries. Fill the paper liners with the batter. Mix 2 Tbsp. shredded coconut with 2 tsp. of sugar and 1/4 tsp. of ground cinnamon. Sprinkle the cherry muffins with the mix. Reduce heat to 350°F (180°C) and bake the muffins on the middle rack in the oven for 25 minutes.

Classic Drink **Baby Piña Colada**

Ingredients for one drink:
*5 1/3 oz. (16 cl) pineapple juice*
*1 1/3 tsp. cream of coconut (canned) or*
  *1 1/3 oz. (4 cl) coconut syrup*
*2 Tbsp. (2 cl) heavy cream*
Garnish:
*1/4 pineapple slice, 1 cocktail cherry,*
*1 cocktail spear*
Plus:
*Ice cubes, blender, large cocktail glass*
*(10 oz. / 30 cl), two drinking straws*

**1** Blend all ingredients in a blender. Put three
or four ice cubes into the glass and pour the
contents of the blender over the ice.

**2** With the help of a cocktail spear, hang the
pineapple slice and the cherry on the rim of the
glass. Serve with the straw.

## Variation:

If you like a creamy sweet taste, you will also
appreciate an **Almond Colada**: Combine 4 oz.
(12 cl) of pineapple juice, 1/3 oz. (1 cl) of freshly
squeezed lemon juice, and 2/3 oz. (2 cl) each of
almond syrup (orgeat) and coconut syrup into
the shaker with four ice cubes. Cap the shaker
and shake vigorously for about 15 seconds.
Pour through the bar strainer into a tall glass
(8 oz. / 24 cl). Serve the drink with two straws.

### Creamy Drink **Tropical Fruit Cup**

Ingredients for one drink:
*2 2/3 oz. (8 cl) pineapple juice*
*2 oz. (6 cl) apricot nectar*
*1 1/3 oz. (4 cl) passion fruit nectar*
*2/3 oz. (2 cl) strawberry syrup*
*2 Tbsp. (2 cl) heavy cream*
Plus:
*Ice cubes, shaker, bar strainer, large cocktail*
*glass (10 oz. / 30 cl), drinking straw*

**1** Combine all ingredients into the shaker with
four ice cubes. Cap the shaker and shake vigorously for about 15 seconds.

**2** Put three or four ice cubes into the glass and
pour the ingredients through the bar strainer
over the ice. Serve with the straw.

### Tropical Drink **Exotic Experiment**

Ingredients for one drink:
*3 1/3 oz. (10 cl) grapefruit juice*
*2/3 oz. (2 cl) freshly squeezed lemon juice*
*2/3 to 1 oz. (2–3 cl) kiwi syrup*
*2/3 to 1 oz. (2–3 cl) banana syrup*
Plus:
*Ice cubes, shaker, bar strainer, tall glass*
*(8 oz. / 24 cl)*

**1** Combine all ingredients into the shaker with
four ice cubes. Cap the shaker and shake vigorously for about 15 seconds.

**2** Pour the contents of the shaker through the
bar strainer into the glass.

## Refreshing Drink **Pink Pelican**
*(left in photo)*

Ingredients for one drink:
*3 1/3 oz. (10 cl) orange juice*
*2 oz. (6 cl) grapefruit juice*
*1/3 oz. (1 cl) freshly squeezed lemon juice*
*1/3 to 2/3 oz. (1–2 cl) grenadine syrup*
*2/3 oz. (2 cl) Rose's lime juice*
Plus:
*Ice cubes, shaker, bar strainer, large cocktail*
*glass (10 oz. / 30 cl), two drinking straws*

1 Combine all ingredients into the shaker with four ice cubes. Cap the shaker and shake vigorously for about 15 seconds.

2 Put three or four ice cubes into the cocktail glass. Pour the contents of the shaker through the bar strainer over the ice. Serve with the straws.

## Garnish:
2 small **strawberry** halves, 4 **honeydew** pieces, 1 cocktail spear

## Tropical Drink **Speedy Gonzales**
*(right in photo)*

Ingredients for one drink:
*2 oz. (6 cl) passion fruit nectar*
*2 oz. (6 cl) grapefruit juice*
*2 oz. (6 cl) banana nectar*
*2/3 oz. Curaçao Bleu syrup*
Plus:
*Ice cubes, shaker, bar strainer, large cocktail*
*glass (10 oz. / 30 cl)*

1 Combine all ingredients in the shaker with four ice cubes. Cap the shaker and shake vigorously for about 15 seconds.

2 Put three or four ice cubes into the glass. Pour the contents of the shaker through the bar strainer over the ice cubes.

## Classic Drink **Pussy Foot**
*(center in photo)*

Ingredients for one drink:
*2 oz. (6 cl) pineapple juice*
*2 oz. (6 cl) orange juice*
*2 oz. (6 cl) grapefruit juice*
*2/3 oz. (2 cl) grenadine syrup*
Garnish:
*1/2 slice pineapple, 1 cocktail cherry,*
*cocktail spear*
Plus:
*Ice cubes, shaker, bar strainer, large cocktail*
*glass (10 oz. / 30 cl), two drinking straws*

1 Combine all ingredients into the shaker with four ice cubes. Cap the shaker and shake vigorously for about 15 seconds.

2 Put three or four ice cubes into the glass. Pour the contents of the shaker through the bar strainer over the ice cubes. Cut the piece of pineapple **(Step 1)** and hang it onto the rim of the glass **(Step 2)**. With the spear add the cocktail cherry to it **(Step 3)**. Serve with the straws.

## Variation:
Instead of grapefruit juice you can also mix this fruity-tangy drink with **lemon juice**. Here's the recipe: For one drink combine 1 2/3 oz. (5 cl) orange juice, 1 oz. (3 cl) each of pineapple juice and lemon juice, and 1/3 oz. (1 cl) of grenadine syrup into the shaker with four ice cubes. Shake vigorously for about 15 seconds. Pour the mixture through the bar strainer into a tall glass (8 oz. / 24 cl) over two or three ice cubes.

Fruity-Sweet Drink **Sugar Love**

*(center in photo)*

Ingredients for one drink:
*3 fresh, ripe strawberries*
*2 2/3 oz. (8 cl) banana nectar*
*1 1/3 oz. (4 cl) peach nectar*
*2 Tbsp. heavy cream*
Garnish:
*1 piece of banana, cocktail spear*
Plus:
*Ice cubes, blender, tall glass (8 oz. / 24 cl)*

**1** Wash and hull the strawberries, and pat them dry. Put them in the blender with the fruit nectars, the heavy cream, and four ice cubes. Blend for about one minute and pour into the glass.

**2** Skewer the piece of banana on the cocktail spear and hang it across the rim of the glass.

Creamy Drink **Coconut Kiss**

*(left in photo)*

Ingredients for one drink:
*2 2/3 oz. (8 cl) pineapple juice*
*1 1/3 oz. (4 cl) orange juice*
*2 Tbsp. (2 cl) each coconut syrup and heavy cream*
Garnish:
*1/4 lemon, shredded coconut in a dish*
Plus:
*Ice cubes, shaker, bar strainer, tall glass (8 oz. / 24 cl), drinking straw*

**1** Run the quarter lemon around the rim of the glass and dip the glass into the dish with the shredded coconut. To remove excess coconut tap the glass lightly.

**2** Combine all other ingredients into the shaker with four ice cubes. Cap the shaker and shake vigorously for about 15 seconds.

**3** Put two or three ice cubes into the glass and pour the contents of the shaker through the bar strainer over them. Serve with the drinking straw.

# Aloha

*(right in photo)*

Ingredients for one drink:
*3 1/3 oz. (10 cl) pineapple juice*
*1 2/3 oz. (5 cl) apple juice*
*1 Tbsp. orange juice*
*1 Tbsp. freshly squeezed lemon juice*
Plus:
*Ice cubes, shaker, bar strainer, tall glass (8 oz. / 24 cl)*

**1** Combine all ingredients in the shaker with four ice cubes. Cap the shaker and shake vigorously for about 15 seconds.

**2** Pour the contents of the shaker through the bar strainer and into the glass.

## *Cocktail Snack*

### *Potato Tortilla*

111

Serves 4–6

Peel four large potatoes and one large onion; then cut the potatoes into small cubes and mince the onion. Over medium heat fry the cubes of potatoes in 2 Tbsp. of olive oil for about five minutes. Add the minced onion. Simmer partly covered for about three minutes. Remove the mixture from the stove, put it into a bowl, and season with a little salt. Beat 8 eggs to a froth, season with salt, and add in the potatoes and onions. In the pan heat 2 Tbsp. of olive oil and pour in the egg and potato mixture. When the eggs are no longer runny, stir a little and shape them into a tortilla. When the tortilla is lightly browned on the bottom, place a plate over the entire pan and turn the pan over. Slide the tortilla back into the pan and finish cooking until done. Let it cool and cut it into small squares. Put a toothpick into each square and serve.

## Summer Drink **Tipsy Passion Fruit**
*(right in photo)*

Ingredients for one drink:
*5 oz. (15 cl) passion fruit nectar*
*2/3 oz. (2 cl) freshly squeezed lemon juice*
*2/3 oz. (2 cl) black currant syrup*
*1/3 oz. (1 cl) almond syrup (orgeat)*
Garnish:
*1 orange slice, 1 cocktail cherry*
Plus:
*Ice cubes, shaker, bar strainer, large cocktail glass (10 oz. / 30 cl), drinking straw*

**1** Combine all ingredients into the shaker with four ice cubes. Cap the shaker and shake vigorously for about 15 seconds.

**2** Put three or four ice cubes into the glass. Pour the contents of the shaker through the bar strainer over the ice. Cut the orange slice in half and hang it on the rim of the glass with the cocktail cherry. Serve the drink with the straw.

## Tropical Drink **Cocomint**
*(center in photo)*

Ingredients for one drink:
*2 2/3 oz. (8 cl) orange juice*
*2 2/3 oz. (8 cl) pineapple juice*
*2 tsp. (2 cl) freshly squeezed lemon juice*
*2/3 oz. (2 cl) green peppermint syrup*
*2/3 oz. (2 cl) coconut syrup*
Garnish:
*1 spring fresh mint, 1 cocktail cherry, cocktail spear*
Plus:
*Ice cubes, shaker, bar strainer, large cocktail glass (10 oz. / 30 cl), drinking straw*

**1** Combine all ingredients except the mint and the cocktail cherry in the shaker with four ice cubes. Cap the shaker and shake vigorously for about 15 seconds.

**2** Put three or four ice cubes into the glass and pour the contents of the shaker through the bar strainer over the ice. Wash the sprig of mint, shake it dry, and add it to the drink. Put the cocktail spear through the cherry and hang it on the rim of the glass. Serve the drink with the straw.

## Tart Drink **Black Currant Shake**
*(left in photo)*

Ingredients for one drink:
*4 2/3 oz. (14 cl) black currant nectar*
*2/3 oz. (2 cl) freshly squeezed lemon juice*
*1/3 oz. (1 cl) cane syrup*
*1 very fresh egg yolk*
Garnish:
*1 lemon slice, 1 cocktail cherry, cocktail spear*
Plus:
*Ice cubes, shaker, bar strainer, tall glass (8 oz. / 24 cl)*

**1** Combine all ingredients in the shaker with four ice cubes. Cap the shaker and shake vigorously for about 15 seconds.

**2** Put two or three ice cubes into the glass. Pour the contents of the shaker through the bar strainer over the ice.

**3** Cut the lemon slice in half. Put the spear through the lemon and the cocktail cherry. Hang them over the rim of the glass.

## Fruity Drink **Lucky Driver**
*(right in photo)*

Ingredients for one drink:
**2 2/3 oz. (8 cl) orange juice**
**1 1/3 oz. (4 cl) passion fruit nectar**
**2/3 oz. (2 cl) freshly squeezed lemon juice**
**2/3–1 oz. (2–3 cl) grenadine syrup**
Plus:
**Ice cubes, shaker, bar strainer, tall glass**
**(8 oz. / 24 cl)**

**1** Combine all ingredients in the shaker with four ice cubes. Cap the shaker and shake vigorously for about 15 seconds.

**2** Pour the contents of the shaker through the bar strainer into the glass.

## Creamy Sweet Drink **Police Control**
*(center in photo)*

Ingredients for one drink:
**2 2/3 oz. (8 cl) pineapple juice**
**2/3 oz. (2 cl) coconut syrup**
**2/3 oz. (2 cl) chocolate syrup**
**1 Tbsp. heavy cream**
**1 Tbsp. whipped cream**
**1/3 oz. (1 cl) grenadine syrup**
Plus:
**Ice cubes, shaker, bar strainer, old-fashioned**
**glass (5 oz. / 15 cl)**

**1** Combine the pineapple juice, the coconut syrup, the chocolate sauce, and 1 Tbsp. heavy cream in the shaker with four ice cubes. Cap the shaker and shake vigorously for about 15 seconds. Pour the mixture through the bar strainer into the glass **(Step 1)**.

**2** With a spoon add a dollop of whipped cream to the drink **(Step 2)**. Drizzle grenadine syrup over the whipped cream **(Step 3)**.

## Tangy Drink **Sports Fan**
*(left in photo)*

Ingredients for one drink:
**2 2/3 oz. (8 cl) pineapple juice**
**2 2/3 oz. (8 cl) grapefruit juice**
**1 Tbsp. freshly squeezed lemon juice**
**2 Tbsp. almond syrup (orgeat)**
Plus:
**Ice cubes, crushed ice, shaker, bar strainer,**
**large cocktail glass (10 oz. / 30 cl), drinking**
**straw**

**1** Combine all ingredients in the shaker with four ice cubes. Cap the shaker and shake vigorously for about 15 seconds.

**2** Fill the glass about halfway with crushed ice. Pour the contents of the shaker through the bar strainer over the ice. Serve with the straw.

## *Cocktail Snack*

### *Bread and Scrambled Eggs*

Serves 8
Whisk 12 eggs with 1 tsp. salt, 4 1/4 oz. (1/8 L) milk and 1/2 tsp. each of mild paprika and black pepper. In a pan, heat 2 Tbsp. (30 g) butter, add the egg and milk mixture, and thicken over medium heat. Rinse two bunches of chives, snip them into tiny pieces, and sprinkle them over the still moist scrambled eggs. Prepare the eggs on a plate and let them cool slightly. In the meantime, cut a small round loaf of bread (approx. 18 oz. / 500 g) horizontally in half. Butter both sides. Line the lower half of the loaf with 4 slices of ham. Add the scrambled eggs. Cover the entire layer with the upper half of the bread and cut into 8 pieces (wedges).

116

### Summer Drink **Passionata**

Ingredients for one drink:
**1 lime**
**2 tsp. raw brown sugar**
**2 oz. (6 cl) passion fruit nectar**
**Ice-cold mineral water to top off**
Plus:
**Crushed ice, pestle, old-fashioned glass
(5 oz. / 15 cl), two short drinking straws**

**1** Wash the lime in hot water, dry it, and quarter it. Put it into the glass and sprinkle it with the sugar. Crush the lime with the pestle and pour the passion fruit nectar over it.

**2** Fill the glass with crushed ice and pour the water over it. Stir thoroughly and serve with the straws.

### Tart Drink **Orange Splash**

Ingredients for one drink:
**2 oz. (6 cl) orange juice**
**2/3 oz. (2 cl) pineapple juice**
**2/3 oz. (2 cl) freshly squeezed lemon juice**
**1 1/3 oz. (4 cl) ginger ale**
**Ice-cold mineral water to top off**
Plus:
**Ice cubes, shaker, bar strainer, tall glass
(8 oz. / 24 cl)**

**1** Put the juices into the shaker with four ice cubes. Cap the shaker and shake for about 15 seconds.

**2** Pour the contents of the shaker through the bar strainer into the glass over two or three ice cubes. Pour in the ginger ale and the mineral water.

### Garnish:

Peel a **lemon slice** halfway around so that there is still a lemon twist attached. Cut the slice partially in the middle and hang it on the rim of the glass.

## Classic Drink **One Jule**

Ingredients for one drink:
*1 lime*
*2/3 oz. (2 cl) Rose's lime juice*
*Ice-cold mineral water to top off*
Plus:
*Crushed ice, pestle, old-fashioned glass*
*(5 oz. / 15 cl), two short drinking straws*

**1** Wash the lime in hot water, dry it, and quarter
it. Put it into the glass and crush it with the
pestle. Add the lime juice.

**2** Fill the glass with crushed ice and pour
mineral water over it. Stir thoroughly and serve
with the straws.

## Substitutions:

To make **Ipanema**, the sister drink to **One Jule**:
For one cocktail, wash one lime in hot water,
dry it, and quarter it. Put the quarters into an
old-fashioned glass (5 oz. / 15 cl) and sprinkle
them with 2 tsp. raw brown sugar. Crush the
lime with the pestle. Fill the glass about halfway
with crushed ice. Pour 1 oz. (3 cl) of lime juice
over it and stir. Top with clear lemonade.

117

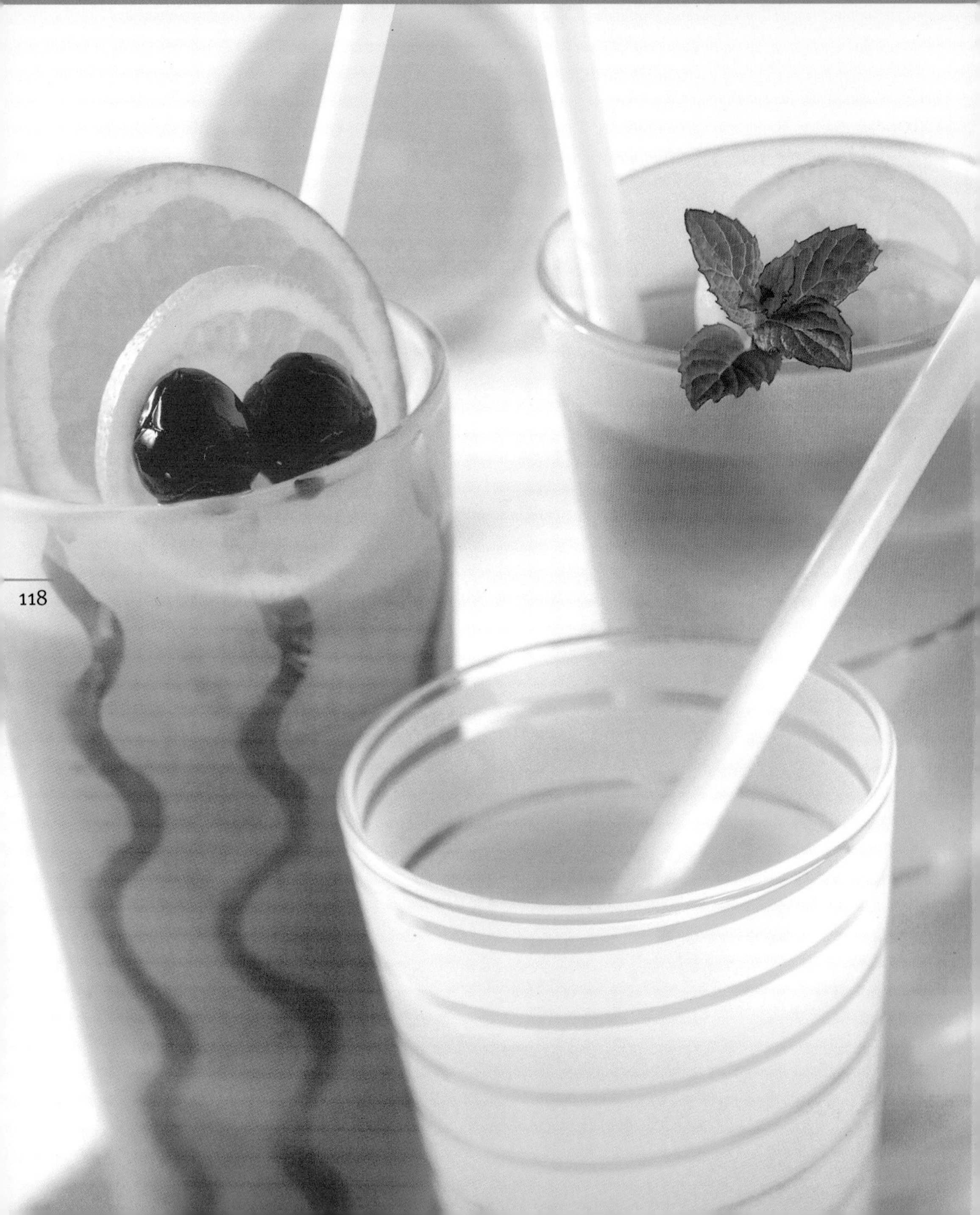

## Refreshing Drink **Iced Mint**
*(right in photo)*

Ingredients for one drink:
*5 oz. (15 cl) cold black tea*
*2/3 oz. (2 cl) freshly squeezed lemon juice*
*1 1/3 oz. (4 cl) peppermint syrup*
Garnish:
*2 lemon slices, 1 sprig fresh mint*
Plus:
*Ice cubes, large cocktail glass (10 oz. / 30 cl),*
*drinking straw*

1 Fill the glass about halfway with ice cubes.
Pour in the tea, the lemon juice, and the peppermint syrup. Stir thoroughly.

2 Put the lemon slices into the drink. Wash the
sprig of mint, shake dry, and put it into the
drink. Serve the drink with the straw.


## Fruity Drink **Indian Lover**
*(center in photo)*

Ingredients for one drink:
*2/3 oz. (2 cl) freshly squeezed lime juice*
*1 1/3 oz. (4 cl) orange juice*
*3 1/3 oz. (10 cl) instant iced tea*
Plus:
*Ice cubes, tall glass (8 oz. / 24 cl), drinking*
*straw*

1 Put two or three ice cubes into the glass.
Pour in the lime juice, the orange juice, and the
iced tea.

2 Stir thoroughly and serve the drink with
the straw.


## Summer Drink **Fruit Tea**
*(left in photo)*

Ingredients for one drink:
*5 oz. (15 cl) black tea*
*1 1/3 oz. (4 cl) orange juice*
*2/3 oz. (2 cl) freshly squeezed lemon juice*
*1 1/3 oz. (4 cl) grenadine syrup*
Garnish:
*One orange and lemon slice each,*
*2 cocktail cherries*
Plus:
*Ice cubes, large cocktail glass (10 oz. / 30 cl),*
*drinking straw*

1 Fill the glass about halfway with ice cubes.
Add the tea, the orange and lemon juices, and
the grenadine syrup. Stir thoroughly.

2 Put the orange and lemon slices into the
drink. Put a cocktail spear through the cocktail
cherries and hang them on the drink. Serve with
the straw.

## *Cocktail Snack*

### *English Cheese Slices*

Makes 4
Preheat the oven to 400°F (200°C). Put 8 oz.
(1 cup) of shredded cheddar cheese in a pan.
Heat 2 Tbsp. of butter and 4 Tbsp. of light
beer. Whisk the cheese into the liquid. Season
with salt, pepper, 1 tsp. of mustard, and 1 tsp.
of Worcestershire sauce. Over low heat keep
the mixture warm. Toast lightly 4 slices of
white bread, place them on a baking sheet
lined with baking paper, and spread each
slice with the cheese mixture. Bake in oven
(medium rack, 350°F / 180°C) for about
15 minutes.

**Shirley Temple**

*(left in photo)*

Ingredients for one drink:
*1 1/3 oz. (4 cl) passion fruit nectar*
*2 2/3 oz. (8 cl) pineapple juice*
*Ice-cold clear lemonade to top off*
Plus:
*Ice cubes, large cocktail glass (10 oz. / 30 cl)*

**1** Put three or four ice cubes into the glass.
First pour in the passion fruit nectar, then the
pineapple juice; stir thoroughly.

**2** Top off with clear lemonade.


Slightly Tangy **Apple Cooler**

*(center in photo)*

Ingredients for one drink:
*2/3 oz. (2 cl) freshly squeezed lemon juice*
*2/3 oz. (2 cl) grenadine syrup*
*2 2/3 oz. (8 cl) apple juice*
*2 2/3 oz. (8 cl) bitter lemon*
Plus:
*Ice cubes, wineglass or large cocktail glass*
*(10 oz. / 30 cl), drinking straw*

**1** Fill the wine or cocktail glass about halfway
with ice cubes. Pour in the lemon juice, grenadine syrup, and apple juice, and stir thoroughly.

**2** Top with bitter lemon, stir well, and serve with
the straw.


Tangy **Cool Mind**

*(right in photo)*

Ingredients for one drink:
*2 2/3 oz. (8 cl) pineapple juice*
*2/3 oz. (2 cl) freshly squeezed lemon juice*
*2/3 oz. (2 cl) green peppermint syrup*
*Ice-cold tonic water to top off*
Plus:
*Ice cubes, tall glass (8 oz. / 24 cl)*

**1** Put two or three ice cubes into the glass. Pour
the juices and the syrup over them and stir well.

**2** Top off with tonic water and serve.

## Substitutions:

This refreshing summer drink can also be prepared with **bitter lemon**; in this case it will be
slightly sweeter.

121

## Cocktail Snack

### Stuffed Walnut Halves

Makes 30 pieces
Prepare 60 walnut halves. Peel and mince one
small onion, and put it into a bowl. Rinse off
and chop one package of fresh watercress.
Add to the onion together with 5 or 6 oz.
(150 g) of soft cream cheese and 1 tsp. lemon
juice. Season the mixture with salt, pepper,
and cayenne, and stir thoroughly. Put 1 tsp.
of cream cheese on each of 30 walnut halves,
place another walnut half on top, and squeeze
the two walnut halves together.

## Diver's World

Ingredients for one drink:
*1/3 oz. (1 cl) freshly squeezed lemon juice*
*1 1/3 oz. (4 cl) Curaçao Bleu syrup*
*2/3 oz. (2 cl) ginger ale*
*1/3 oz. (1 cl) bitter lemon*
*Tonic water to top off*
Garnish:
*Several stemless red currants, 3 lime slices*
Plus:
*Ice cubes, shaker, bar strainer, tall glass*
*(8 oz. / 24 cl)*

**1** Put the lemon juice and Curaçao Bleu syrup into the shaker with two ice cubes. Cap the shaker and shake for about 15 seconds. Pour the mixture through the bar strainer into the glass.

**2** Add the ginger ale and bitter lemon, top off with tonic water, and stir. Put the currants and the lime slices into the glass and serve.

## Cocktail Snack

### Shrimp on a Spit

Makes 25
Wash and slice horizontally one zucchini (about 7 oz. / 200 g) in cold water. Rinse off about 3 oz. (80 g) of shelled, cooked shrimp and pat them dry. Fold the zucchini slices bookwise in the middle. Stuff each slice with one shrimp and skewer together with a wooden spear. In a frying pan, heat an ample amount of sunflower oil. Fry the shrimp skewers on both sides for about 30 seconds (watch out for spattering!). Remove the shrimp skewers and drain them on a paper towel. Whisk together 1 Tbsp. balsamic vinegar, 1 Tbsp. lemon juice, 1 tsp. chopped dill, salt, pepper, and 1 pinch sambal oelek (Indonesian mixture of chile and salt); beat in 2 Tbsp. olive oil. Drizzle over the skewers.

## Tall Drink **Lovely Long**

Ingredients for one drink:
*1 1/3 oz. (4 cl) orange juice*
*2/3 oz. ( 2 cl) freshly squeezed lemon juice*
*1/3 to 2/3 oz. (1–2 cl) almond syrup (orgeat)*
*Ice-cold ginger ale to top off*
Plus:
*Ice cubes, crushed ice, shaker, bar strainer, tall*
*glass (8 oz. / 24 cl), drinking straw*

**1** Combine the orange juice, the lemon juice,
and the almond syrup into the shaker with four
ice cubes. Cap the shaker and shake vigorously
for about 15 seconds.

**2** Fill the glass about halfway with crushed ice
and pour the contents of the shaker over it.
Top off with ginger ale.

**3** Wash the sprig of mint, shake it dry, and put it
into the glass. Serve the drink with the straw.

## Garnish:

You can prepare this bubbly, fruity drink with an
**almond rim**. In this case, before preparing the
drink, run a quarter-lemon around the rim of the
glass and then dip the rim in a dish filled with
grated almonds. Tap the glass lightly to remove
excess almond.

123

**A** Absinthe
Absinthe Sunset 51
Green Ice Fairy 51
Sazerac 51
**Americano** 52
**Anisette**
Anise Blanc 77
Crocodile 77
Tomato Cocktail 77
**Aperol**
Aperol Sour 79
Fellini 23
Florida 79
**Apollo 8** 67

**B** B 52 73
**Banana Batida** 81
**Banana Liqueur**
Yellow Bird 59
**Beer**
Noble Beer 75
**Bellini** 27
**Berry Limes** 73
**Between the Sheets** 25
**Bittersweet**
Symphony 86
**Bitter Swirl** 75
**Bloody Mary** 18
**Blue Curaçao**
Blue Hour 86
Turquoise 91
**Blue Ocean** 65
**Bordeaux Cobbler** 99
**Bourbon and**
Whiskey
Green Beam 33
Horse's Neck 45
Manhattan 43
Mint Julep 45
Old-fashioned 43
Sazerac 51
Whiskey Fizz
(Substitution) 31
Whiskey Sour 44
**Brandy**
Between the Sheets 25

Brandy Alexander 75
Bull's Eye 83
Fruity Brandy 83
**Brasilic Ale** 80
**Bull's Eye** 83

**C** Cachaça
Banana Batida 81
Brasilic Ale 80
Caipirinha 53
Cherry Lips 54
Frogman 54
Latin Lover 53
Peppermint Patty 53
Wild Thing 55
Woody Woodpecker 80
**Caipirinha** 53
**Caopirovka** 71
**Calvados**
Calvados Sour
(Substitution) 44
Double Apple 57
Red Pleasure 57
Tropical Apple` 57
**Campari**
Americano 23
Bittersweet 85
Campari Cocktail 22
Campari Passion
Fruit 75
C-O-L-L-ision 79
East-West
Connection 99
**Champagne**
Champagne Cocktail 27
Portofino 29
Prince of Wales 29
**Cherry Lips** 54
**Coconut Liqueur**
Bittersweet
Symphony 86
Coco Sunrise 87
Pineapple Batida 75
**Coconut Sunrise** 87
**Coffee Liqueur**
B 52 73

Black Russian
(Substitution) 47
Kahlua Tropical 65
White Russian 47
**Cognac**
Between the Sheets 25
Bull's Eye 83
Matador 83
Prince of Wales 29
Sidecar 25
**C-O-L-L-ision** 79
**Comfort Cooler** 89
**Cosmopolitan** 47
**Crocodile** 77
**Cuba Libre** 39

**D** Daiquiri 38
**Double Apple** 57
**Dream of Peach** 95

**E** East-West Connection 99
**El Presidente** 38

**F** Fellini 23
**Florida** 79
**Florida Comfort** 91
**Frogman** 54
**Frozen Daiquiri** 38
**Frozen Vodka Lemon** 85
**Fruity Brandy** 83
**Fuzzy Navel** 87

**G** Galliano
Golden Dream 59
Harvey Wallbanger 47
Yellow Bird 59
Yellow Chief 58
**Gin**
Gimlet 35
Gin and Tonic 75
Gin Fizz 31
Gin Orange 75
Gin Sour
(Substitution) 44
Golden Bronx
(Substitution) 30

Journalist 31
Long Island Iced
Tea 63
Martini
Apple Martini 35
Dirty Martini 35
Paradise 33
Silver Bronx 30
Singapore Sling 33
Tom Collins 35
White Lady 33
**Golden Bronx**
(Substitution) 30
**Golden Dream** 59
**Grappa**
Green Moon 61
Old Gondolier 61
Sandy's Sofa Surfer 61
**Green Beam** 43
**Green Ice Fairy** 51
**Green Moon** 61
**Green Poison** 67

**H** Happy Apricot 85
**Harvey Wallbanger** 47
**Horse's Neck** 45

**I** Irish Cream Liqueur 73
B52 73
Ireland Orange 91

**J** Journalist 31

**K** Kamikaze 73
**King Midas** 67
**Kir** (Substitution) 27
**Kir Royale** 27
**Kiwi's Fate** 92

**L** Latin Lover 53
**Long Island Iced Tea** 63
**Los Angeles** 47

**M** Mai Tai 37
**Manhattan** 43
**Margarita** 41

124

**Martini**
  Apple Martini 35
  Dirty Martini 35
**Matador** 83
**Mimosa** 28
**Mint Julep** 45
**Mojito** 39

**Noble Beer** 75

**Old-fashioned** 43
**Old Gondolier** 61
**Orange Liqueur**
  B 52 73
  Golden Dream 59
  South Seas 89

**Paradise** 33
**Pear Blue** 95
**Peppermint Patty** 53
**Piña Colada** 37
**Pineapple Batida** 75
**Pisco Sour**
  (Substitution) 44
**Planter's Punch** 37
**Port Fizz**
  (Substitution) 31
**Portofino** 29
**Port Wine**
  Port Fizz
    (Substitution) 31
  Portofino 29
**Pretty in Pink** 71
**Pretty Woman** 29
**Prince of Wales** 29
**Prosecco**
  Dream of Peach 95
  Kiwi's Fate 92
  Pear Blue 95
  Red Kiss 95
  Sparkling Passion
    Fruit 93
  Sweet Ruby 92

**Red Currant Liqueur**
  Refreshing Cassis 89

**Red Kiss** 95
**Red Ocean**
  (Substitution) 65
**Red Pleasure** 57
**Refreshing Cassis** 89
**Rob Roy** 44
**Rum**
  Cuba Libre 39
  Daiquiri 38
  Frozen Daiquiri
    (Happy Hour) 38
  Long Island Iced Tea 63
  Mai Tai 37
  Mojito 39
  Piña Colada 37
  Planter's Punch 37
  Rum Sour
    (Substitution) 44
  Tame Zombie 62
  Yellow Bird 59
  Yellow Chief 58
  Zombie (Variation) 62

**Sandy's Sofa Surfer** 61
**Sangria** (Happy Hour) 62
**Sazerac** 51
**Sex on the Beach** 69
**Sherry**
  Sherry Shandy 97
  Spanish Cream 96
  Summery Sherry 96
**Sidecar** 25
**Silver Bronx** 30
**Singapore Sling** 33
**Southern Comfort**
  Comfort Cooler 89
  Florida Comfort 91
  Manhattan Comfort 43
**South Seas** 89
**Spanish Cream** 96
**Sparkling Passion**
  **Fruit** 93
**Sparkling Wine**
  Bellini 27
  Berry Limes 73
  Kir Royale 27

Noble Beer 75
Pretty Woman 29
Prince of Wales 29
**Strawberry Margarita** 41
**Summery Sherry** 96
**Sweet Ruby** 92
**Swimming Pool** 68
**Swinging Girl** 99

**Tame Zombie** 62
**Tequassis** 65
**Tequila**
  Apollo 8 67
  Blue Ocean 65
  Green Poison 67
  Kahlua Tropical 65
  King Midas 67
  Latin Lover 53
  Long Island Iced Tea 63
  Margarita 41
  Red Ocean
    (Substitution) 65
  Strawberry
    Margarita 41
  Tequassis 65
  Tequila Sour
    (Substitution) 44
  Tequila Sunrise 41
**Tomato Cocktail** 77
**Tom Collins** 35
  Colonel Collins
    (Substitution) 35
  Joe Collins
    (Substitution) 35
  Pedro Collins
    (Substitution) 35
  Ruben Collins
    (Substitution) 35
  Rum Collins
    (Substitution) 35
**Tropical Apple** 57
**Turquoise** 91

**Vodka**
  Apricot Touch 69
  Berry Limes 73

Black Russian
  (Substitution) 47
Bloody Mary 18
Caipirovka 71
Frozen Vodka
  Lemon 85
Harvey Wallbanger 47
Kamikaze 73
Long Island Iced Tea 63
Los Angeles 47
Pretty in Pink 71
Sex on the Beach 69
Swimming Pool 68
Vodka Fizz
  (Substitution) 31
Vodka Lemon 75
Vodka Martini 35
White Cloud 71
White Russian 47

**White Cloud** 71
**White Lady** 33
**White Russian** 47
**Wild Thing** 55
**Wine**
  Bordeaux Cobbler 99
  East-West
    Connection 99
  Happy Apricot 85
  Kir (Substitution) 27
  Sandy's Sofa Surfer 61
  Sangria (Happy
    Hour) 99
  Swinging Girl 99
**Woody Woodpecker** 80

**Yellow Bird** 59
**Yellow Chief** 58

**Zombie** (Variation) 62

125

*An index of all nonalcoholic drinks is on page 127.*

# Index by Taste

**Aromatic Drinks**
Bordeaux Cobbler 99
Kahlua Tropical 65
Matador 83
Prince of Wales 29
White Lady 33

**Creamy Drinks**
Anise Blanc 77
Apollo 8 67
Brandy Alexander 25
Golden Dream 59
Piña Colada 37
Spanish Cream 96
Swimming Pool 68
White Cloud 71
White Russian 47

**Dry and Semidry Drinks**
Champagne Cocktail 27
Journalist 31
Kir Royale 27
Manhattan 43
Martini 35

**Fruit Drinks**
Apricot Touch 69
Bellini 27
Berry Limes 73
Blue Ocean 65
Cherry Lips 54
Comfort Cooler 89
Crocodile 77
Fellini 23

Florida Comfort 91
Fruity Brandy 83
Harvey Wallbanger 47
Ireland Orange 91
King Midas 67
Kiwi's Fate 92
Latin Lover 53
Los Angeles 47
Planter's Punch 37
Portofino 29
Pretty in Pink 71
Pretty Woman 29
Sex on the Beach 69
Singapore Sling 33
Sparkling Passion
  Fruit 93
Strawberry
  Margarita 41
Sweet Ruby 92
Tame Zombie 62
Tequila Sunrise 41
Woody
  Woodpecker 80

**Refreshing Drinks**
Absinthe Sunset 51
Aperol Sour 79
Blue Hour 86
Bull's Eye 83
Cuba Libre 39
Dream of Peach 95
Frozen Vodka
  Lemon 85
Green Beam 43

Green Ice Fairy 51
Happy Apricot 85
Mint Julep 45
Mojito 39
Pear Blue 95
Sherry Shandy 97
South Seas 89
Swinging Girl 99
Tropical Apple 57
Turquoise 91

**Strong Drinks**
B 52 73
Kamikaze 73
Long Island Iced Tea 63
Mai Tai 37
Old-fashioned 43
Old Gondolier 61
Red Pleasure 57
Sazerac 51
Wild Thing 55
Yellow Bird 59
Yellow Chief 58

**Sweet Drinks**
Banana Batida 81
Coco Sunrise 87
Green Poison 67
Peppermint Patty 53
Red Kiss 95

**Tangy Drinks**
Americano 23
Between the Sheets 25

**Bittersweet**
  Symphony 86
Bitter Swirl 85
Campari Cocktail 22
C-O-L-L-ision 79
Daiquiri 38
Double Apple 57
East-West
  Connection 99
Florida 79
Gimlet 35
Green Moon 61
Horse's Neck 45
Paradise 33
Sandy's Sofa Surfer 61
Silver Bronx 30
Tomato Cocktail 77
Tom Collins 35

**Tart Drinks**
Brasilic Ale 80
Caipirinha 53
Caipirovka 71
Frogman 54
Gin Fizz 31
Margarita 41
Refreshing Cassis 89
Sidecar 25
Summery Sherry 96
Tequassis 65
Whiskey Sour 44

## Cocktail Snacks

Aromatic Olives 22
Bacon Plums 35
Baked Munchies 95
Blue Cheese Spread 62
Bread and Scrambled
  Eggs 115
Cheese and Crackers 93
Cheese Spears 25

Cherry Muffins 105
Chicken Salad 33
Cucumber Sandwiches 30
English Cheese Slices 119
Feta Pockets 97
Fig Morsels 79
Guacamole 89
Meatballs 51

Papaya Morsels 58
Potato Tortilla 111
Ranch House Pecans 57
Salsa Mexicana 41
Shrimp Spears 122
Stuffed Walnuts 121
Trout Pockets 71
Tuna Crostini 61

# Index of Nonalcoholic Drinks

**Alice** 103
**Aloha** 111
**Apple Cooler** 121

**Baby Piña Colada** 106
**Banana Nectar**
  Speedy Gonzales 109
  Sugar Love 111
**Bitter Swirl** 85
**Black Currant**
  **Shake** 113

**Car Driver** 103
**Cherry Juice**
  Dragon Heart 105
**Cinderella** 103
**Cocomint** 113
**Coconut Kiss** 111
**Cool Mind** 121
**Cream**
  Alice 103
  Baby Piña Colada 106
  Cinderella 103
  Coconut Kiss 111
  Police Control 115
  Sugar Love 111
  Tropical Fruit
    Cup 107

**Diver's World** 122
**Dragon Heart** 105

**Exotic Experiment** 107

**Fruit Tea** 119

**Grapefruit Juice**
  Cinderella 103
  Exotic
    Experiment 107
  Pink Pelican 109
  Pussy Foot 109
  Speedy Gonzales 109
  Sports Fan 115

**Iced Mint** 119
**Indian Lover** 119
**Ipanema** 117

**Lemonade**
  Apple Cooler 121
  Cool Mind 121
  Diver's World 122
  Shirley Temple 121
**Lovely Long** 123
**Lucky Driver** 115

**Matador** 83
**Mineral Water**
  Ipanema 117
  One Jule 117
  Orange Splash 117
  Passionata 116

**One Jule** 117
**Orange Splash** 116
**Orange Juice**
  Alice 103
  Car Driver 103
  Cocomint 113
  Fruit Tea 119
  Indian Lover 119
  Lovely Long 123
  Lucky Driver 115
  Orange Splash 116
  Pink Pelican 109
  Pussy Foot 109
  Spring Awakening 105
  Tempting Orange 105

**Passionata** 116
**Passion Fruit Nectar**
  Lucky Driver 115
  Passionata 116
  Speedy Gonzales 109
  Tempting Orange 105
  Tipsy Passion Fruit 113
**Pineapple Juice**
  Alice 103
  Almond Colada 106
  Aloha 111
  Baby Piña Colada 106
  Cinderella 103
  Cocomint 113
  Coconut Kiss 111

Cool Mind 121
Police Control 115
Pussy Foot 109
Shirley Temple 121
Sports Fan 115
Tropical Fruit Cup 107
**Pink Pelican** 109
**Planter's Punch** 37
**Police Control** 115
**Pussy Foot** 109

**San Francisco** 47
**Shirley Temple** 121
**Speedy Gonzales** 109
**Sports Fan** 115
**Sugar Love** 111
**Swimming Pool** 68

**Tea**
  Fruit Tea 119
  Iced Mint 119
  Indian Lover 119
**Tempting Orange** 105
**Tipsy Passion Fruit** 113
**Tropical Fruit Cup** 107

127

## The Author

**Alessandra Redies** specialized in German and general studies in Munich, Germany, and has worked in the cookbook division of a German publisher since 2000. While writing this book, she devoted lots of attention to the question of "shaken or stirred?," converted her kitchen into a bar, and regaled friends and colleagues with cocktails from classics to ones she created herself.

## The Technical Advisor

**Till Caspari** has been working as a bartender in an American bar in Darmstadt, Germany, for nine years. What started out as a part-time job while he studied history and philosophy turned into a profession. Since early 2002 he has been a co-owner of "Hillstreet No. 73," where he started out as a manager.

## The Photographer

**Michael Brauner** worked as a photo assistant for famous photographers in France and Germany. Since 1984, after finishing his photography studies in Berlin, he has been working as a freelance photographer. His individual style is appreciated everywhere, in advertising as well as in many well-known companies. In his studio in Western Germany he turns recipes into dream photos.

## The Translator

**Eric Bye, M.A.,** is a freelance foreign language translator who lives in Vermont and translates works from German, French, and Spanish into English.

## Photo Credits

P.3: Teubner Foodphoto; all others: Michael Brauner

Published originally under the title *Cocktails*, in the series *Einfach Clever* © 2002 by Gräfe and Unzer Verlag GmbH, München

English translation © Copyright 2005 by Barron's Educational Series, Inc.

German edition by: Alessandra Redies
Photography by Michael Brauner
English translation by Eric A. Bye

All rights reserved. No part of this book may be reproduced in any form, by photostat, microfilm, xerography, or any other means, or incorporated into any information retrieval system, electronic or mechanical, without the written permission of the copyright owner.

*All inquiries should be addressed to:*
Barron's Educational Series, Inc.
250 Wireless Boulevard
Hauppauge, New York 11788
**http://www.barronseduc.com**

Library of Congress Catalog Card No. 2005926990

ISBN-13: 978-0-7641-5869-8
ISBN-10: 0-7641-5869-4

Printed in China

9 8 7 6 5 4 3 2 1